Distinctively ✠ *Catholic* ✠

AN EXPLORATION OF CATHOLIC IDENTITY

Daniel Donovan

PAULIST PRESS
New York / Mahwah, N.J.

Cover design by Cynthia Dunne

Biblical texts are cited according to the New Revised Standard Version and the documents of Vatican II from *Vatican Council II*, edited by Austin Flannery (Collegeville: The Liturgical Press, 1979). Other conciliar statements are taken from *Decrees of the Ecumenical Councils*, edited by Norman P. Tanner (Washington: Georgetown University Press; London: Sheed and Ward Limited, 1990).

Library of Congress Cataloging-in-Publication Data

Donovan, Daniel, 1937–
    Distinctively Catholic : an exploration of Catholic identity / Daniel Donovan.
        p.   cm.
    ISBN 0-8091-3750-X (alk. paper)
    1. Catholic Church—Doctrines. I. Title.
BX1754.D615 1997
282—dc21   97-24108
                                                                            CIP

Published by Paulist Press
997 Macarthur Boulevard
Mahwah, New Jersey 07430

Printed and bound in the
United States of America

Contents

For Stephanie

May she come with time to love and live the faith
in which as an infant she was baptized.

Introduction

A few years ago I was asked to develop an introductory course on Catholicism for the Christianity and Culture Program at St. Michael's College at the University of Toronto. Given the different ways in which the word *catholic* has been used in the Christian tradition, the course might have dealt with a variety of topics. In its broadest sense the term appears in the creed along with "one, holy, and apostolic" as a distinguishing mark of the church of Christ. All Christians who recite the creed apply in one way or another all of these words to themselves and to their own communities. *Catholic* is also used on occasion to point to certain elements shared by a number of churches—such as episcopacy, apostolic tradition, and a strong sacramental system—that distinguish them from more Protestant or evangelical forms of Christianity. In this sense one hears about catholic and evangelical emphases in the Anglican tradition. Finally Catholicism refers to the worldwide Catholic Church, united through its bishops with and under the pope, the bishop of Rome. It was in this sense that the word was proposed as a title for the course and it is in this sense that it will be largely used in the present book, even though much of what is said in it can be applied to other Christian communities as well.

Catholicism, thus understood, is much more than a creed or a set of doctrines. It is a living community of faith, a community with its own distinctive rituals and structures, its own patterns of individual and collective religious life. It is a community that has experienced a long and complex history, one reaching back now almost two thousand years. In the course of that history it has grown and developed; it has encountered and entered into complex relationships with a variety of cultures and historical situations, cultures

1

and situations it has both influenced and been influenced by; it has known periods of extraordinary vitality and expansion, as well as periods of crisis and decline. What is true of the past remains true of the present. History continues. In recent decades, for example, Catholicism has become in a new way a truly world church, more and more at home in all the great cultural traditions of humanity. Its numerical center of gravity is shifting from the Western and First Worlds to the Third World, especially to Latin America and Africa. In Asia, in spite of remaining a relatively small minority, it is marked in a number of places by important efforts to enter into more positive and creative relationships with local cultures.

It was an awareness of the richness and complexity of Catholicism and its tradition that led me to dedicate the first semester of the course to history. As much as I hoped that the students would come away with a sense of some of the key figures, decisive turning points, and important movements in church history, the emphasis was less on an overall narrative and more on those distinctive practices, structures, attitudes, and ideas that increasingly over the centuries came to mark Catholic identity. The focus in dealing with the early centuries, for example, was on the development of creeds and liturgies and on the work of ecumenical councils. The treatment of the medieval period underlined the role of the papacy, the importance of monastic and other forms of religious life, and the significant implications for theology and Christian intellectual endeavors more generally of the development of the universities. The last several weeks of the first semester looked at the ways in which Catholicism responded to the challenges first of the Protestant Reformation and then of the Enlightenment and of its social, political, and intellectual offshoots.

The first three weeks of the second semester dealt with Vatican II and its major themes and tried to situate the council's efforts at church renewal within the broader sweep of Catholic history. The final ten weeks offered, in the form of a theological reading of the creed, an overview of a contemporary Catholic understanding of human life and God, of Christ and the Spirit, of the church and its inner life and mission.

When asked more recently to give a series of lectures under the same general title, Catholicism, instead of trying to condense the whole range of topics covered by the course, I opted to focus on what I call distinctive features, distinctive characteristics, of the Catholic experience of Christianity. It is these features or characteristics that constitute the focus of the present book.

From a purely phenomenological point of view, Catholicism is a part of a wider religious reality, Christianity. Catholics share much that is central to their faith and life with countless other believers. All serious Christians, for example, believe in God, not in some vague kind of way, but precisely as God has turned to us in Jesus Christ. Christian faith is simultaneously theocentric and christocentric. It affirms the reality of the creator God, the one who is the beginning and the end, the ground and the goal, the source of meaning, of all that is. What is most distinctive about the Christian understanding of God is rooted in faith in Jesus of Nazareth as the one who has brought salvation and revelation in a definitive way into the midst of human history. The God in whom Christians believe is a saving God, a God who has been revealed in the person and teaching, the life and destiny of Jesus. More than simply one more prophet or religious genius, Jesus is God's Word incarnate, God's Son in human form. John's gospel sums up the centrality of Jesus for Christian faith in God with the simple phrase "who sees me, sees the Father."

According to the almost universal conviction of Christians, faith in Jesus is impossible without the gift of his Spirit. It is the Spirit, the Spirit of both God and of the risen Christ, who continues the work of Jesus among us. The Spirit unites us with Christ and transforms us from within, thus enabling us to become true disciples. Christian faith in God, Jesus, and the Spirit has been articulated in the great creeds of the church; it is the faith into which almost all Christians are baptized and which as adult believers they affirm. It is essential to Christian and therefore to Catholic identity.

As important as this common core of Christian faith is to all believers, the present book is not concerned primarily or directly with offering an exposition of it. Inevitably and in a variety of contexts it will evoke certain aspects of it, but its major concern is elsewhere. It wants to draw attention to certain emphases and characteristics of Catholicism that to a significant degree have influenced and continue to influence the way in which Catholics experience and think about their faith. Catholic experience obviously varies from age to age and from culture to culture. There are, however, certain constant elements, certain basic themes, and it is these that the book is intended to highlight.

One of the major developments in Catholicism since Vatican II has been its commitment to the ecumenical movement. The council recognized the efforts already being made by Anglicans, Orthodox, and Protestants to further the cause of Christian unity and saw them as reflecting the will of Christ and as being inspired by the Holy Spirit. It affirmed the desire of the Catholic Church to become part of the process and called for the setting up of bilateral and multilateral dialogues between Catholics and other Christians. In spite of inevitable difficulties along the way, enormous progress has been made in this area in the post-conciliar period. Many theological studies today self-consciously and quite rightly attempt to be ecumenical in their approach. Some are even written from what is called a post-denominational perspective. While recognizing the importance of ecumenical concerns, the present book focuses on Catholic issues. The traditional church divisions remain and in all probability will continue to do so for some time to come. It is important, moreover, that we bring to dialogue a real appreciation for our own traditions, for their strengths and their weaknesses. The dialogue should help us to deepen and to share what is positive and to learn to recognize and to overcome what is negative in our respective heritages.

When one begins to reflect on what is distinctively Catholic, on what is characteristic about the Catholic experience of Christianity, one thing that comes immediately to mind is an emphasis on community, a concern for the church as such. More than many Christians, Catholics tend to be conscious of themselves as members of the church. It is something that influences every aspect of their religious life. Catholicism has always taken seriously the surprising fact that the church itself is part of the creed. What is at stake here is not simply a pragmatic or sociological phenomenon but a reality of faith. The first chapter will try to understand the role attributed to the church in the Catholic tradition and to suggest some of its implications.

Catholicism, as already suggested, is not only in itself a historical reality, it also takes history seriously. It has an acute awareness of its debt to, and responsibility for, the past. It is rooted in particular historical events, the events that constitute the history of Israel and in a special way those that make up the life and destiny of Jesus. It has a deep concern with tradition, with the safeguarding and handing on of what was once given in the whole event of Christ. At the same time, it knows that history continues and sees itself as called to contribute in a significant way to its unfolding. As a community of faith, a community rooted in the saving activity of Christ, Catholicism knows itself to be tending toward fulfillment, its own and that of all human history. Some of the many facets of the historical dimension of Catholicism will be addressed in the second chapter.

Catholics are conscious that it is a shared faith more than anything else that binds them together into a religious community. That faith is central to Christian life, all Christians would agree. It is by faith that we are justified, by faith that we are brought into a living and life-giving relationship with Christ and the Spirit. While affirming the absolute necessity of such faith, Catholicism seems to have a heightened sense of what might be called the objective nature of faith. Faith is not just and not primarily a subjective attitude. It involves a content, something concrete and specific that has been revealed to us by God in Jesus Christ. It offers a vision of God, the world, and the meaning and destiny of human life. In the revelation that is ours in Christ, there is a deep and precious truth that needs to be understood, articulated, defended, handed on, brought into creative and challenging relationship with changing historical and cultural contexts. It is this conviction that has led in Catholicism to an emphasis on such things as creeds and orthodoxy, theology, and the teaching authority of popes and bishops. These and related topics are included in the third chapter under the title "A Community of Faith."

Central to the experience of Catholics is the role that ritual and liturgy play in their religious lives. Baptism and eucharist, weddings and funerals, are critical moments in the life of the

Catholic community. Here Catholicism expresses itself, becomes aware of itself in the most explicit and concrete of ways. At the heart of the liturgy are the seven sacraments. The emphasis given to them suggests that for Catholics religious experience tends to be not only communal but also mediated. Catholicism has an acute sense that we encounter God not just in the inwardness of our hearts but in and through one another, in and through bread and wine, oil and water, ritual and proclaimed word. Catholicism is a sacramental religion. Chapter four will try to get at the theological roots as well as the implications of that affirmation.

The Catholic Church has always given a certain priority to structures, to organization, to the ordained ministry, to what traditionally has been called the hierarchy. Although Catholicism is a community, it is not an amorphous community. It recognizes in the ordained ministry, and especially in the threefold structure of deacon, priest, and bishop, a divinely given element of its identity. Such offices do not exist for themselves but are there to build up the community, to protect and hand on and proclaim its faith, to preside over its ritual. For Catholics, church structure culminates in the college of bishops and in the pope as its head and the center of unity. Over the centuries the pastoral leadership exercised by the ordained ministry has taken many forms. It is clearly facing new challenges and possibilities today. Chapter five will attempt to show why, no matter what comes out of present and future debates in regard to this area, Catholicism will continue to cherish the contribution of ordained leadership.

There is a certain tension, even a paradox, in the phrase *Roman Catholicism*. The word *catholic* comes from a Greek root meaning "universal" or "according to the whole." It was used for the first time in a Christian context by Ignatius of Antioch, a bishop and martyr, around the year 115 in a letter he wrote to believers at Smyrna in Asia Minor. "Where the bishop is to be seen, there let all his people be: just as wherever Jesus Christ is present, we have the Catholic Church." Initially *Catholic* seems to have referred to the large church as opposed to small heretical sects, to the large church made up of the many small churches spread throughout the Mediterranean world but living in a genuine community of faith with one another. Gradually the word came to take on a second and more qualitative sense. It suggested the openness of the church to all peoples and cultures. More recently the word has come to evoke the kind of diversity that should mark a church that is meant to be at home in the various traditions and cultures that are a part of our global village.

The other word in the phrase *Roman Catholicism* is much more specific. It points to a particular city, a particular church, a particular bishop. For Catholics the papacy is in a very special way the center and focus of unity for the universal church. As its full name suggests, Catholicism is called to be both one and many, both united and enriched by real diversity. The struggle to maintain the balance between these two values is part of Catholicism's distinctiveness. It will be dealt with in chapter six.

St. Paul reminds us that we bear the treasure of Christian faith and of the gift of the Spirit in earthen vessels. The church as a community of believers is exposed to failure and inadequacy, to mediocrity and sin. This is true of every Christian church, of every religious community, of every individual believer. Catholicism has its own special temptations, temptations tied up to a large degree with what is most distinctive about it. Church leaders and people need to be aware of such things and to struggle against them. Chapter seven will look briefly at "Catholic Temptations, Catholic Renewal."

No one of the above themes by itself can adequately suggest what is distinctive about the Catholic tradition. Many of them in fact are to be found to different degrees in other Christian churches and communities as well. The juxtaposition of all of them, however, does give some insight into what is characteristic about the Catholic experience of Christianity. The different themes are obviously interrelated. What is said in the first chapter about community, for example, will be deepened and become more specific in what is said about creeds and ordained ministry, about liturgy and ritual. So, too, for most of the other themes that are to be treated. It is their organic interrelationship that helps to account for the rich and varied and yet profoundly unified phenomenon that is Catholicism.

My own understanding and appreciation of Catholicism has been shaped by years of theological study and teaching but also by personal experience. Born in 1937 in Toronto into an Irish Catholic family, I was both raised in the pre–Vatican II period and experienced firsthand the kind of emphases and preoccupations that at that time often marked minority Catholic communities in the English-speaking world. Theological studies at Laval University in Quebec City between 1958 and 1962 introduced me to a very different kind of Catholicism. During those years the culture and the public life of the province of Quebec were still profoundly influenced by Catholic attitudes and values and by Catholic organizations. The fact that the language of the Quebec church was French provided me a key to the religious thought and culture that for centuries had been so central a feature of the life of France.

Between 1963 and 1965 I was a student at the Biblical Institute in Rome. The fact that Vatican II was then in session created for me a special opportunity to experience the worldwide nature of the church. Although as a young priest I was very much on the edge of what was happening, the drama of the council could not help but have a significant impact on my developing a sense of Catholicism. Here were bishops from every continent and from almost every country debating and making decisions about important issues in regard to the nature of the church and its mission; here, too, were St. Peter's and the other Christian monuments of Rome teaching anyone who was willing to learn from them about the long and in so many ways extraordinary history of Catholic Christianity.

The pursuit of a doctorate in theology took me to Münster in northern Germany, where I was taught by a remarkable group of Catholic theologians that included Karl Rahner, Joseph Ratzinger, Walter Kasper, and Johann Baptist Metz. In many ways the faculty of theology at Münster at that time was the most exciting and creative center for Catholic theology in Europe. The city and its surrounding area were deeply marked by Catholicism and by its religious, cultural, and intellectual history. It was a powerful and formative experience for a young priest from Canada. It deepened and broadened in many ways my already growing appreciation of Catholicism.

If these are key elements in my background and education, my experience over the last twenty-five years in Toronto and at

St. Michael's College has been that of many North American Catholics. The church and the world have changed in our lifetime and so has our experience of our religion. Some of the changes have been positive and liberating. Some have been more challenging. Overall, North American culture has become more secular. Many people have lost confidence in their religious traditions and in church leadership and have drifted away from the practice of their religion. Some have been drawn to more personal and private forms of religious life.

One of my hopes in writing the present book is to reawaken in Catholics a sense of the wealth of their own heritage. Another is to introduce others who may be approaching Catholicism for the first time to the same reality. Catholicism has a wonderfully rich history and tradition, rich in humanity and in religious and Christian experience and values. The way that each person lives all of this varies to some degree depending on age, education, and ethnic and cultural background. And yet there are certain things that Catholics have in common. The more general reflections of the first seven chapters of the book will take on more concrete form in the eighth and final chapter entitled "Being Catholic Today." The treatment there will not be exhaustive but it will suggest some implications for the life of each and every one of us of those things that are distinctive of the Catholic experience of Christianity.

CHAPTER ONE

An Emphasis on Community

Contemporary North American culture, as homogeneous in so many ways as it obviously is, has become increasingly individualistic in regard to religious and ethical questions. Pluralism in these areas is not only taken for granted, it is cherished as a positive good. The markedly secular nature of modern public life tends, moreover, to push religion into the sphere of the private and the personal. Religion, the conventional wisdom suggests, is something that concerns individuals, something that they are free to accept or reject and to work out in ways that best suit their particular sensitivities and needs.

Although this kind of religious individualism is most obvious in New Age and analogous movements, it clearly affects some Christians as well. Among the more vital and successful of Christian groups in recent years have been those that have put an emphasis on personal religious experience. Whether on television or from local pulpits, evangelical preachers eloquently proclaim a deeply personal religion, involving a personal conversion to Christ and a personal experience of forgiveness and salvation. They rarely speak of the church except perhaps as a community of like-minded believers that recent converts might join in order to find reinforcement and support for their newfound faith.

Even Catholics seem to have been touched by the growing individualism of the age. The move from the old inner-city, largely ethnic parishes to the suburbs has weakened for some their sense of religious belonging. For others the debates about birth control and more recently about the role of women in the church, including women's ordination, have made their relationship to the Catholic community more ambivalent. The simple fact of attending the Sunday eucharist in a rather large parish with people with whom one usually has little or no contact is turning out to be for many an inadequate means for renewing or deepening their sense of the community of faith.

Whatever the causes of contemporary religious individualism, it is profoundly at odds with much that is central to the traditional understanding of Catholic identity. The community of believers, the church, is at the heart of the Catholic experience and articulation of Christian faith. One of the most serious challenges facing Catholics today is the need to renew and deepen their understanding of what might be called the ecclesial nature of their faith and to find forms and structures in which they can live and foster it.

If one wants to renew one's thinking on this question, as with so many others, the starting point has to be the person and teaching of Jesus. One can only appreciate his message and the significance of his life, however, against the background of the Judaism within which he was born and from which he inherited so much that was central to his language, thought patterns, and religious sensitivities.

The story of the Bible is above all the story of a people, the people of Israel. The story is told from a specifically religious point of view. The Israelites became a people because God called them and formed them into one. God saved them out of slavery in Egypt and at Sinai established with them a covenant, a kind of contract or agreement. The basic thrust of the covenant is evoked by a phrase that comes back as a kind of refrain throughout the Bible: "I will be your God and you will be my people."

The Bible tells the story of the way the covenant relationship was lived out. It speaks of Israel's fidelities and failures, triumphs and defeats. In and through the ups and downs of the history of the people, God remains present among them—protecting, admonishing, forgiving, and punishing them. The biblical account is full of strong individuals, people like Abraham and Moses and the prophets; their role, however, is always presented in relationship to the larger community. Abraham and Sarah are called to become the parents of a great nation. Moses leads his people through the wilderness and acts as an intermediary for them with God. The prophets are not isolated ascetics or religious geniuses but often very ordinary individuals from quite different backgrounds who are inspired to speak God's word to their compatriots. It may be a word of consolation or of condemnation, of hope or of trust, but it is always God's word, and it is always addressed to the people as a whole and to their leaders so that they might respond to it and do God's will.

As the centuries passed, Israel's religious faith, rooted as it always was in the founding events of the exodus and of Sinai, turned more and more to the future. People hoped and prayed that God would establish the kingdom in a definitive way on earth and that Israel and in some manner all of creation might be brought to fulfillment. Sometimes this vision of a better future included a messianic figure who would be the instrument of God's renewing activity.

It was against this background that Jesus preached the near approach of the reign or kingdom of God. In some sense it was already present in him; it broke through in his healing activity and in his reaching out to the poor and to the marginalized. His ministry seems to have been restricted to the people of Israel. The twelve whom he chose from his disciples and whom he associated in a special way with his activity were symbolic of the renewal of the twelve tribes of Israel, which was thought to be a part of the final coming of God's kingdom. The very notion of Messiah, as indeed of all the other traditional Jewish categories that were applied to Jesus, is inseparable from the establishment or reestablishment of God's people.

Explicit Christian faith was born with the experience of the resurrection of Jesus and with the gift of the Pentecostal Spirit. The apostles and others saw in the resurrection a vindication of all that Jesus had said and done. The cross, far from being a disaster and a defeat, was in fact a prelude to triumph and a means of salvation. The resurrection revealed that God was indeed with Jesus and that through him God was offering people forgiveness and reconciliation and the possibility of a new and renewed covenant. The gift of the Spirit was the sign and the firstfruits of the new age that was dawning. The prophecy of Jeremiah about a new and spiritual covenant was being fulfilled (Jer 31:31–34).

Jesus invited individuals to follow him, not in isolation but as members of the community of his disciples. Those who left father and mother in order to be with him discovered that they were being welcomed into a new family, that they had become brothers and sisters of one another and of Jesus.

THE EARLY CHRISTIAN COMMUNITY

The sense of joining a community, of becoming part of a family, was integral to the Christian conversion experience from the very beginning. The Acts of the Apostles offers a somewhat stylized version of what the first Christian sermon must have been like. It is Pentecost, and Peter proclaims to the crowds gathered in Jerusalem the story of Jesus and especially of his death and resurrection. In raising Jesus from the dead, "God had made him both Lord and Messiah" (Acts 2:36). Moved by Peter's preaching, some of those listening to him ask what they should do. "Repent," he says, "and be baptized... in the name of Jesus Christ so that your sins may be forgiven; and you will receive the gift of the Holy Spirit." The text goes on to say that "about three thousand persons were added," added, that is, to the existing community symbolized by the twelve and those gathered with them for the outpouring of the Spirit. From the beginning baptism is not simply a ritual that relates individuals to the saving grace of Christ, it is a means by which they enter into the community of faith. Receiving forgiveness and the gift of the Spirit are inseparable from becoming members of the church.

Acts says of those who were baptized on Pentecost that "they devoted themselves to the apostles' teaching and fellowship, to the breaking of bread and the prayers" (Acts 2:42). Although different interpretations of the passage are possible, it clearly underlines not only the strong community sense that marked early Christianity but also the kind of activities and attitudes that defined the nature of its shared life. The community is a community of faith. One enters it because one has responded positively to the initial preaching of the gospel. Growth in faith demands a continual reflection upon, and deepening appreciation of, the teaching of the apostles. The phrase "the breaking of bread" is used elsewhere in Acts to refer to the eucharist. It would seem that from the beginning it was central to Christian community life. The reference to the prayers underlines yet again the deeply religious nature of the new community. People prayed with and for one another at the eucharist and at other times. Such mutual concern was motivated by and found expression in what the present text calls "fellowship." The Greek word here is *koinonia;* it suggests sharing, communion, having things in common. Acts, a few verses further on, says that the first Christians in Jerusalem were so caught up in the common life in the Spirit that marked their being together that they were inspired to share things with one another. "All who believed were together and had all things in common; they would sell their possessions and goods and distribute the proceeds to all, as any had need" (Acts 2:44–45).

The kind of emphasis on community and community life that one discovers in the Acts of the Apostles can be found in a more or less explicit fashion in the other writings of the New Testament as well. St. Paul offers a striking example in this regard. More is known about him than about any other of the first generation of Christians. He had a strong sense of himself and of his special vocation and gifts. He tells us of his conversion experience and of his conflicts, trials, and suffering; he offers more than a hint of deep and personal religious experiences that helped to give direction to his life and preaching. Paul's special vocation was to preach the gospel to the Gentiles and to be the founder of a number of churches among them. As much as he tended to work more or less on his own, he manifested in all that he did a real and abiding concern for the unity of the church. As tenaciously as he defended his understanding of the freedom of the gospel, for example, and even confronted Peter when he believed that Peter was undermining it (Gal 2:11–21), Paul was always careful to foster good relations with the church of Jerusalem and with the other apostles.

THE BODY OF CHRIST

At the heart of Paul's preaching was a call and a challenge to people to personal conversion and to a personal commitment to Christ. He spelled out for his hearers how Christ had loved them and had died for them and was now inviting them into a profoundly personal relationship with him. For all this stress on the individual and the personal, however, Paul had an acute sense of the role of the church. The relationship of believers to Christ is inseparable from their relationship to one another. If baptism plunges a person into the death and resurrection of Jesus, it is also a rite of initiation by which one enters the church. Paul seems to have been the first Christian thinker to have thought of the church as the body of Christ. The use of the analogy of the human body to suggest the dynamic and interdependent relationships of a social group was not new with him. It was a commonplace among the Stoics and other ancient thinkers. Distinctive of Paul's use of the image was his insistence that the community of believers is the body of Christ. Christians, through faith and baptism, belong to Christ. Having been baptized in his name, they have received the gift of his Spirit, they have been clothed with his life, they now live in him. The one Spirit, which has been poured out on them, binds them together and melds them into a single body.

The notion of the church as the body of Christ receives a new depth of meaning when it is brought into relation with the eucharist. Paul deals explicitly with the eucharist in two passages in 1 Corinthians, in both of which he suggests elements of what might be called a eucharistic ecclesiology. Chapter 10 treats of a problem related to the attitude and practice of Christians in regard to meat sacrificed to idols. In this context Paul speaks of "the bread that we break" and "the cup of blessing that we bless" as a sharing *(koinonia)* in the body and blood of Christ. The "fellowship" or "communion" that was so cherished in early Christianity is more than a purely human thing. It is rooted in the communion that all believers have in Christ. That the two kinds of relationship are themselves interrelated is underlined by Paul when he evokes an analogy that will have enormous impact over the centuries. "Because there is one bread, we who are many are one body, for we all partake of the one bread" (1 Cor 10:17). The same idea is reflected in what may well be the earliest eucharistic prayer that we have, one contained in a late first- or early-second-century Jewish Christian document known as the Didache: "As this broken bread was scattered over the mountains, and when brought together became one, so let your church be brought together from the ends of the earth into your kingdom" (Didache, 9). The bread made from the many grains of wheat and then broken and shared among believers is a symbol and a sacrament of the common life that is theirs in Christ.

In chapter 11 of 1 Corinthians, Paul finds himself obliged to address an abuse that has arisen in the local community. It seems that when people gathered to celebrate the Lord's Supper those who were well off manifested a considerable insensitivity in regard to the poor. At the time the eucharist was still celebrated in conjunction with a meal. Those who could afford it ate and drank their fill, while others were left hungry. The failure in community life that this represents undermines and in some sense renders vain the eucharistic proclamation of the death of Christ. Contempt for the community of the faithful and especially for its weakest members is incompatible with a genuine eucharistic celebration. The intended fruit of the eucharist is a deepened awareness on the part of the community of itself as the body of Christ.

Like Jesus himself, the writers of the New Testament are steeped in the language and imagery of Israel and of the Jewish scriptures. In their use of traditional categories they sometimes seem to suggest that the church has replaced Israel as God's chosen people and that the establishment of the new covenant means the end of the covenant given through Moses. Paul knows that this is not the case. For him God's promises once made are not withdrawn, nor will the covenant once given be broken from God's side. Israel remains God's people and in the mystery and wisdom of God they too will be brought to salvation (see Rom 9–11). One needs to keep these convictions of Paul in mind in reading what other New Testament books have to say about the church as the heir of the promises made to Israel. They speak of the church as the new Israel, as the new people of God. What is important for our purposes is the basic message that all such texts are trying to communicate: Christianity has nothing to do with individualism. It continues the pattern that God established with Israel. Although membership in the church is not by birth but rather by faith and personal conversion, Christianity, like Israel, stresses the role of the community. The church as church is part of God's plan; it is a recipient and means of God's saving activity.

THE PRIESTHOOD OF THE FAITHFUL

Vatican II has brought back into the consciousness of Catholics the idea of the priesthood of the faithful. The classic New Testament text in regard to this theme is found in the first letter of Peter. It does not affirm that the baptized are individually priests but rather that together they constitute a holy priesthood, a priestly people. In many ways the letter reads like a baptismal homily. At the very least it is full of baptismal themes. Believers are encouraged to come to Christ, "a living stone," and to allow themselves to be "built into a spiritual house, to be a holy priesthood, to offer spiritual sacrifices acceptable to God through Jesus Christ" (1 Pt 2:4–5). The background here is the covenant of God with Israel. Like the Israelites, Christians are "a chosen race, a royal priesthood, a holy nation, God's own people" (1 Pt 2:9). The last phrase is developed with a reference to the prophet Hosea: "Once you were not a people, but now you are God's people; once you had not received mercy, but now you have received mercy" (1 Pt 2:10, cf. Hos 2:23).

The message of 1 Peter could hardly be more explicit. As God called the Israelites of old and made of them his chosen people, so now in Christ, God invites all races and nations to enter through faith and baptism into a new people of God, a people called in all that they are and do to offer praise and thanksgiving to God for the gift that has been poured out on them. Together the baptized are to be built up into a spiritual temple in which through Christ they are able to offer to God the perfect sacrifice of lives lived according to the divine will.

THE CHURCH IN GOD'S PLAN OF SALVATION

The letters to the Ephesians and the Colossians, whether written by Paul or by disciples steeped in his thought, carry the New Testament message about the church and its central place in

God's plan for human salvation to its climax. Both documents talk about the mystery of God, a mystery hidden from all eternity but now revealed in Christ. It is a mystery of salvation, "a plan for the fullness of time, to gather up all things in him [Christ], things in heaven and things on earth" (Eph 1:10). God's plan of salvation embraces all of creation. Christ's person and activity have cosmic significance. According to a famous hymn conserved in Colossians he is "the image of the invisible God"; "all things have been created through him and for him"; "through him God was pleased to reconcile to himself all things, whether on earth or in heaven, by making peace through the blood of his cross" (Col 1:15–20). As in the prologue of John's gospel and in the opening verses of the letter to the Hebrews, the coming of Christ is rooted in the eternal plan of God and has ramifications for all of reality. The church is part of that plan. It has a meaning and a role in God's eyes that go far beyond the individuals that make it up. Throughout history the church continues in the world the mission of Christ. The mystery revealed in him has taken a new form: it is now Christ in us (Col 1:27). If the church, as Paul had already affirmed, is the body of Christ, then Christ, these letters add, is its head. His life, his Spirit, is poured out upon it, enabling it to grow and develop and to come to the full stature of life and love that God intends for it.

The author of Ephesians addresses himself to Gentile converts and reminds them of the grace that is theirs in Christ. They "who once were far off have been brought near by the blood of Christ." He is their peace; he has broken down the dividing wall of hostility that separates Jews and Gentiles and has reconciled the two groups to one another in a single body. Both are now "members of the household of God, built upon the foundation of the apostles and prophets, with Christ Jesus himself as the cornerstone." Together they constitute "a holy temple in the Lord," "a dwelling place for God" (Eph 2:11–22).

These texts represent what might be called an ecclesiology from above. They see the church not so much as a community of individual persons who have responded to the call of the gospel but rather as an almost heavenly reality intended by God from all eternity and now brought into the world through Christ. Just as

Jesus himself comes from God and fulfills God's plan of salvation, so the church, the community of believers, is called into existence not just to ensure the salvation of its individual members but to continue Christ's work, to be a vital part of God's plan for universal salvation. The church has a mission rooted both in the mission of Jesus and in the creative and redemptive will of the eternal God.

The New Testament Greek word for church is *ekklesia.* Its root suggests both an act of calling and the resultant coming together of people in response to a call. In the latter sense it points to what might be described as the phenomenology of church. Church happens when individuals gather together and form community in response to the preaching of the gospel. A traditional definition of the church is the Latin phrase *congregatio fidelium,* a congregating or assembling of believers. The more active sense of call points beyond the believers to the one who calls them. Ultimately it is God who invites people to faith through Christ and in the power of the Spirit. The church is a community of believers, but it is also and inseparably the church of God, of Christ and of the Spirit.

THE CHURCH IN THE CREED

It is quite clear that in the New Testament the idea of the community of the faithful, the church, is never something purely human, something simply created by believers to meet their religious and other needs. At some levels it looks like that, but its real meaning and significance have to be sought elsewhere. The church is a religious reality with a role in God's plan of salvation. As with Christ, its true significance only becomes evident when it is seen against the broadest possible horizon. The church as the community of the redeemed reaches back to Abel, as the great teachers and bishops of early Christianity liked to put it, and forward to the end of time, when, according to the Book of Revelation, it will be transformed into the heavenly Jerusalem.

The religious significance of the church is brought out by the fact that it is included in the creed. The Apostles' Creed, for example, affirms belief in "the holy, catholic church": the so-called

Nicene Creed expands the formulation somewhat so that the phrase now reads "the one, holy, catholic, and apostolic church." All the great creeds of Christianity are trinitarian in structure. They organize the content of Christian faith around the three persons of the Trinity: Father, Son, and Spirit. The opening article affirms faith in God as the creator of all that is. Then comes a mention of the Son, the redeemer, who became flesh as Jesus of Nazareth. Reference is also made to his death and resurrection and to their saving significance. The third section speaks of the Holy Spirit, the sanctifier, the Lord and giver of life. It is in the third part that the church is mentioned alongside of the forgiveness of sins, the resurrection of the dead, and life everlasting. All these things are related in some way to the work of the Spirit. It has been suggested that the earliest form of this section of the creed was "I believe in the Holy Spirit in the holy church."

If creation is the fundamental presupposition and abiding ground for the Christian vision of reality, Christian faith focuses in a special way on the person and destiny of Jesus. In him God's Son has become flesh and in doing so, and above all in undergoing suffering and death and experiencing the triumph of the resurrection, has brought about definitive and universal salvation. What he achieved once and for all in his life among us continues to be operative in the world through the action of the Spirit. Present to all of creation, the Spirit is present in a special way within the church of Christ, animating it and making it an instrument of the risen Christ's saving activity. Although we do not believe in the church as we believe in God or Christ or the Spirit, it is an object of faith. The human community that we can see and the history of which we can study, as weak and hopelessly inadequate and even sinful as it is, embodies a divine reality and is called to play an indispensable role in God's plan for human reconciliation.

Catholicism has always taken seriously the divine dimension, the divine mission of the church. To become a Christian is never just a personal decision and action. It involves entry into a community of faith in which people, yes, will be supported and encouraged in their religious life but in which also they are invited to contribute in some fashion to the community's life and mission.

If both the New Testament and the creeds underline the

corporate nature of Christianity and the deep religious and theological meaning of the community of faith, the ways in which people have experienced that community over the centuries have varied dramatically. In our own day, as the world itself changes along with the place of the church in it, one of the great challenges facing Catholicism is to find concrete forms and ways in which believers can experience in a genuinely human fashion the community dimension of their faith and have their understanding and appreciation of it renewed.

DIFFERENT EXPERIENCES OF COMMUNITY

For almost the first three hundred years of its history the church was largely made up of relatively small, predominantly urban communities spread throughout the countries bordering on, and east of, the Mediterranean. Christians at the time regularly found themselves at odds with both the dominant cultures that surrounded them and the political structures within which they had to live. Although there were only occasional empire-wide persecutions, believers were aware of the possibility of local upheavals that could bring disadvantage, suffering, and even death. Some time before the end of the second century, in order to ensure that those joining the church in such conditions were indeed ready for the commitment they were making, a process of initiation was developed that lasted anywhere from six months to two or three years. Most of those who were baptized in the first centuries were adults. Their faith and their ability to lead the Christian life had to be nourished and tested. They had to be gradually introduced to the life of the community they were about to join. The catechumenate, as the process was called, presupposed and reinforced the sense of community that many took for granted. Given the size of most of the local churches, believers tended to know one another relatively well and were able to support and challenge one another in their efforts to live the Christian life. Each community had its own bishop, who regularly presided over its major liturgical celebrations including baptism and the Sunday eucharist.

Once Christianity was given legal status by the Roman

emperors and then became the official religion of the empire, all this began to change. Increasing numbers of people joined the church, and before long infant baptism became the normal practice. As the communities grew in size, the bishop was no longer able to play the role that he once did. What are now known as parishes began to develop and over them a presbyter or priest presided and provided many of the liturgical services once restricted to the bishop. By the medieval period the whole of Western society had to a large degree become at least nominally Christian. People took membership in the church for granted. As long as the society that surrounded the church remained predominantly Christian, people could not help but have a sense of the corporate nature of their faith. The church was everywhere; its values permeated public life; its great feast days were the occasion for public celebrations and holidays.

With time, the division between clergy and laity and the separation of their respective spheres of activity became more marked. The very word *church* tended to be used to describe the ordained, especially bishops and pope. The liturgy was seen as a clerical activity that the laity attended. The situation obviously varied from place to place and from period to period. But it is probably no exaggeration to say that, although Christianity was firmly anchored in the rural and urban life of European society, the church as the religious activities of the clergy was increasingly seen as a kind of institution standing over against the world of the laity. People went to church to be taught their religion and to receive the grace of the sacraments. The liturgy, however, was not experienced as an act of the community but as something that was done for it by the clergy.

The place where the early Christian experience of a lived community of faith was primarily kept alive in the medieval period was in the monastic and religious tradition. To study the history of that tradition is to be struck by how much the development of monastic and religious life was tied up with the desire to renew and deepen a sense of Christian community. If the first monks went off to the desert in the pursuit of a life of asceticism and prayer, many among them soon began to form communities, the ideal of which was directly inspired by the experience of the early church as this was reflected in the first chapters of the Acts of the Apostles. Both St. Basil, one of the fathers of Eastern monasticism, and St. Augustine, the author of writings that would decisively influence the development of religious life in the medieval West, insisted on the importance of community. People were to live together in order better to foster and to exercise the Christian virtue of love. Members of monastic and religious orders were conscious of trying to live the ideal of the church with a particular intensity. In doing so they offered an example to, and acted as a leaven for, the wider church community.

It is not by chance that both contemplative and active religious orders have played such an important role in the history of Catholicism. Their search for community, their sense of common purpose, and their awareness of a common mission are inspired by and reflect something that is central to the Catholic experience and understanding of Christianity in general. In our own day organized religious life is undergoing both a crisis and a renewal. New forms of religious communities are beginning to develop. Whatever the future will bring in this area, it seems highly probable that in some form or other religious communities will continue to be inspired by the Catholic vision and in their turn will continue to be instruments of renewal for Catholicism.

VATICAN II'S RENEWED VISION OF CHURCH COMMUNITY

It was only really during the course of the council's first session in the fall of 1962 that the bishops gathered in Rome were able, under the leadership of people such as Cardinals Suenens and Montini, to focus on the church as the central theme of their deliberations. Although they were motivated in coming to this decision by a number of questions, there was a widespread consensus about the need for Catholics in general to renew their sense of the church and of its inner life and mission, and their understanding of the roles of clergy, religious, and lay people in it. The council became for many of those involved in it an experience of the kind of relationships that are meant to mark the life of the church. The almost twenty-five hundred bishops who attended the four fall plenary sessions from 1962 to 1965 had come from all parts of the globe. Most of them did not know one another. Many in fact had little contact even with other bishops from their own countries and regions. The council became an experience of community, not only of the bishops but also of the community of the churches that they represented. This experience became part of the data that flowed into the debate on collegiality. Bishops are not just isolated church leaders responsible for their respective dioceses; they belong to a worldwide college or group who together have a shared responsibility, with and under the pope, for the universal church. What the bishops were rediscovering was something almost as old as Christianity. The early church spoke of the *order* of bishops, a word that suggests the special bond that is meant to exist among them and the common responsibility they share.

The bishops' rediscovery of community among themselves spilled over into the way, for example, they thought about the corporate nature of the priesthood or the "presbyterium," as they began to call it, as well as into the way they developed their basic understanding of the church. Although Vatican II has seemed to many people to represent something new, in many ways what it said, especially in this area, was quite traditional. It represented a return to values and insights that in many cases had been widely held in the early church. It was almost as if the bishops, recognizing that the kind of intertwining of church and society that marked medieval Christendom had come to an end, decided to turn to early Christian experience for insight into how they might renew the life of the church in a pluralistic and increasingly secular world. The various conciliar documents appeal again and again to the patristic period as well as to the New Testament for their inspiration.

Drawing upon some of the same images that we have already evoked, Vatican II spoke of the church as the people of God, the body of Christ, and the temple of the Spirit. It insisted above all on the religious nature of the church. It is not primarily an institution or a legal structure but a community of faith rooted in the very mystery of God as turned to us in Christ and in the Spirit. The bishops were particularly concerned to reawaken in lay people a sense of the active role that they are called to play in the church's life and mission. All believers together constitute the church.

The most central image for the church at Vatican II, the one to which a whole chapter of the *Dogmatic Constitution on the Church,* the council's fundamental doctrinal document on the church, is dedicated, is that of the people of God. No image could make it more immediately evident that when we are talking about church we are not talking primarily about buildings or institutions or structures or even the hierarchy, but rather about people, about human beings gathered together in a community of faith. Although some people have reacted in the post-conciliar period against the use of this image for the church, fearing that it might be understood in a purely sociological way, or that it might be used to oppose laity and clergy, the image is so rich in biblical overtones that it is crucial that it not be forgotten or abandoned. The people whose story is at the heart of the Bible exist as a people only because God has intervened in their history and molded them into a people. The great law of their life is the covenant. They are God's people and as such have a mission in the world that is unlike that of other people.

The image of the people of God is complemented and enriched by the image of the body of Christ. If Israel is God's people and if in some sense all of humanity is called to the same destiny, then the church is that part of God's people that has embraced Jesus as God's revelation and salvation and that through the gift of the Spirit has become his body. The language of the body of Christ emphasizes the way in which Christians belong to and receive their life from Christ. The organic nature of the image, especially when allied with the idea of Christ as the body's head, underlines the community of life that defines the church.

The church is simultaneously and inseparably a visible and historical phenomenon that can be perceived and studied and a mystery of grace and inner life. It is the Spirit that binds believers together with Christ and with one another. In the years since the council, theologians and church leaders have given a particular emphasis to what is sometimes called an ecclesiology of communion. Church is all about *communio, koinonia*. At all its different levels and in a variety of ways it involves a sharing of life among those who are a part of it. We are, as Paul put it, all members one of another. What makes this relationship unique is that it is rooted in that koinonia or communion that we all have with God, in Christ, through the Spirit. The ultimate basis and the deepest ground of Christian community is the dynamic relationship of love and self-giving that marks the inner life of the Trinity.

THE COMMUNITY AND THE RENEWAL OF THE LITURGY

Although the council took a number of steps to give concrete form to the Catholic sense of community, the most visible and perhaps the most effective ones were in the area of liturgy. The preconciliar liturgy had much about it that was attractive. When celebrated with the kind of dignity and reverence that it called for, it created an atmosphere of mystery and awe. Here something truly important was taking place, and Catholics felt privileged to be a part of it. The emphasis, however, was on the role of the clergy. The Mass was widely understood as something that the priest did for others. It seemed perfectly natural to focus on private devotions even while attending the community eucharist.

Building on the liturgical renewal of the previous half-century, the bishops at Vatican II endorsed a profoundly renewed theology of the liturgy. The liturgy is an act of the whole church, not just of the clergy. It is even more significantly an act of the whole Christ, head and members together. In the liturgy Christ is in the midst of the community, the individual members of which are united with one another and with him through the Holy Spirit. Although the bishop or priest celebrant has an essential and distinctive role to play in the eucharist, it is something in which the whole community is actively involved. We offer it together and in doing so bring ourselves and our lives and unite them with the sacrifice of Christ. Our communion in his offering deepens our relationship with him and with one another.

This fundamental theological vision was at the root of the specific liturgical reforms for which the council called. If the liturgy is an act of the whole community, then it is important that everyone present be helped to participate actively and in a conscious and knowing way in it. In order for this to be a real possibility, it was decided that the ritual should be simplified and made more accessible and in key parts translated into the vernacular. The positive response to the first efforts at translation motivated Paul VI to approve the use of the vernacular for the whole of the eucharistic celebration as well as for all of the other sacramental and liturgical rites of the church. The rapid development in recent decades of the use of lay readers and lay ministers of communion has reinforced the sense of church ritual as a corporate act. For many Catholics, the liturgy well prepared and reverently celebrated has been a privileged means by which their sense of the community dimension of their faith has been deepened and reinforced.

In order to underline the active role that all members of the church are called to play in the liturgy, the council brought back to Catholic consciousness the traditional idea of the priesthood of the faithful. In the period following the Protestant Reformation there was a tendency on the part of both Catholics and Protestants to think of the universal or general priesthood as being in opposition to the ordained or ministerial priesthood of priests and bishops. Vatican II moved beyond such polarization and emphasized the positive relationship that exists between the two forms of participation in the one priesthood of Christ. All the baptized share in Christ's priesthood. They are enabled through the gift of the Spirit to live the kind of life of obedience to God and self-giving love that constituted the sacrifice of Jesus. It is this that they bring to the eucharist and, in union with other believers and with the ordained priest, they offer with, through, and in Christ to the glory and praise of God.

Vatican II, as 1 Peter before it, insists on the corporate nature of the priesthood of the faithful. Nowhere is this dimension of the common priesthood more eloquently expressed or profoundly experienced than in the gathering of the community for the eucharist. The same gathering brings home that the priesthood of the ordained is ministerial in nature; it exists to minister to and to build up by word and sacrament and pastoral leadership the priesthood of the faithful.

THE CHURCH AS SACRAMENT

In relation to the liturgy Vatican II introduced another way of thinking about the church to which we will come back in a later chapter. It merits a first mention here, however, because it evokes in a simple but striking way how central the church is to the Catholic understanding of Christianity. After centuries in which the word *sacrament* was used in the Catholic tradition primarily to refer to seven specific ritual actions, the council had recourse to it to describe the nature and mission of the church. Although some thought of this use as vague and novel, it, once again, goes back to early Christianity.

We saw above how the letters to the Ephesians and Colossians speak of the divine mystery hidden from all eternity that has now been revealed in Christ. Colossians affirms that the revelation process continues in the church. The mystery, it says, is Christ in us. The Greek word used here for mystery was translated in an early Latin version of the New Testament as *sacramentum*. Bishops and teachers in the Western church came thus to speak of God's plan of salvation as a sacrament. Christ as the heart and center of that plan was seen as the fundamental sacrament. In calling the church a sacrament in a secondary sense, they suggested that it has to be seen as in some sense continuing the work of Christ. It is this idea that Vatican II wanted to underline. The church as church is more than simply a gathering of individual believers. As a community of faith it is and is called to be a sign and an instrument of Christ's saving activity. For his contemporaries Jesus was a visible and tangible embodiment of God's saving presence. As the risen Christ he makes use of the humanity of the community of faith to prolong the visible dimension of his presence in the world. The church is a sacrament of Christ and of Christ's Spirit. By becoming members of the church individuals share in its sacramental nature and mission.

Whether one consults the Bible, the creeds, or the documents of Vatican II, it is quite clear that the Christian tradition understands itself to be at odds with all extreme forms of individualism. Human beings as created by God are fundamentally social. They are made to be in relation with one another, and it is only as such that they are able to fulfill their fundamental vocation. The

Christian doctrine of the Trinity gives an added dimension of meaning to the social implications of the teaching that human beings are made in God's image and likeness. The biblical story builds on this affirmation of the Book of Genesis and insists that as much as God invites individuals into relationship with God, they are called at the same time into community and to a life of service to one another and to everyone in need. God made a covenant not with a series of individuals but with a people and eventually with humanity itself. In keeping with God's intent, Christ came not to save souls out of the world but to begin a process of human renewal. He is, as Paul puts it, the new Adam, the beginning of a new and renewed human race. Salvation from God in Christ is meant for all people and all ages. Human history is moving toward fulfillment in God. In the interim, we live in the time of the church. As the community of those who have believed in Christ and who have been baptized in his death and resurrection, the church shares in his mission and ministry; it gives visible expression to his continuing involvement in human life. The council invited Catholics to renew their sense of the church and to become more actively involved in its life and mission. In the pluralistic and secular kind of world in which we live, this will only be possible to the extent that concrete and humanly convincing forms of community life are developed, forms that foster a real experience of the communal nature of the Christian faith. The renewal of the liturgy has gone a long way in helping this process along.

PERSONS IN COMMUNITY

Vatican II's emphasis on the ecclesial or community dimension of Catholic life is complemented by a healthy appreciation for the dignity and responsibility of individuals. Not everything about the modern preoccupation with the individual and especially with individual human rights is at odds with the Christian tradition. Christian faith in fact has always insisted on personal responsibility and personal faith. In its documents on religious liberty and on the church in the modern world, the council emphasizes in particular the unique value of freedom and the special dignity of conscience. Faith and religious practice can never be coerced. Truth and goodness can never by imposed. If the Catholic emphasis on community is opposed to much of modern individualism, it is not at odds with but rather presupposes what might be called a balanced personalism. The human person made in the divine image has a dignity and rights that need to be respected. Authentic community can only flourish when mature persons come together in freedom for a common goal. In a Christian context that presupposes a common faith and a common commitment.

The theme of human rights and human dignity is central to what is called Catholic social doctrine. Church leadership in the course of the twentieth century has slowly developed a body of teaching about political, social, and economic issues facing the contemporary world. The key in many ways to this doctrine is a conviction about the unique value of human life. Human beings are more important than things or structures or ideologies. The human person must not be seen as a mere instrument for the pleasure or the gain of another. What is true of society at large must obviously be true to an even greater degree within the community of the church.

The teaching about the fundamental dignity of all is reinforced and deepened in regard to the inner life of the church by the conviction that the Spirit of Christ is poured out not only on church leaders but on all the baptized. Vatican II recalled the teaching of St. Paul about the charisms or gifts of the Spirit. There exists in the church a rich variety of such gifts. What is important is that people should be encouraged to develop them and to put them to the service of the common good. The community of the church will only be what it is meant to be when such gifts are recognized and nourished and when those who are endowed with them are stimulated to find creative and positive ways to use them.

A GOD-WILLED COMMUNITY

The purpose of this first chapter has been to draw attention to the fact that over against all forms of modern individualism, including religious individualism, Catholicism puts an emphasis on community, on what might be called the ecclesial dimension of Christian faith and life. Just as we live in other aspects of our lives in dependence on, and not in isolation from, one another, so we receive and live our faith in a community context. This community is not something secondary. Nor is it something that believers create for their own purposes, no matter how spiritual and elevated these might be. It is something that is willed by God and that continues in a visible way the mission and ministry of Jesus Christ. The church is a profoundly religious reality, a creation of the risen Christ and of the Spirit. Believing in Christ and becoming a member of the church are inseparable for Catholics. Catholics recognize the saving presence of God to people everywhere. God's offer of salvation is universal. It can be realized in individuals who have never joined the church or even heard of Christ. Yet those who do respond explicitly to the gospel message and become baptized are not to interpret their experience in an individualistic way. They are called to become active members of the church and to contribute to its life and mission. Their own shared life of faith and worship, of mutual service and commitment to justice, is meant to be a sacrament, a sign and vehicle, of the saving, healing presence of Christ and the Spirit in the midst of human history.

CHAPTER TWO

The Importance of History

If human life of its very nature is social, it is also radically temporal. We live in time. Past, present, and future are very much a part of our experience of ourselves and of the world. Although at different periods of life we may experience these three dimensions of time in different ways and emphasize differently their relative significance, all three are central to our identity.

We come out of and are dependent on the past. Who our parents were, when and where we were born, our relation to our siblings, the influences we were exposed to as children, our education or lack of it, the friends we made, the professions or jobs we chose or fell into, the person we did or did not marry—these and a host of similar things have had a real impact on who and what we have become and how we see ourselves and respond to the events and challenges that confront us today.

As profound as our debt to the past is, however, we tend most of the time not to think about it. Our focus is the present. The passing days and years bring their moments of joy and pleasure as well as of pain and concern. These command our attention and our response. The intensity of present experience or perhaps just the weight of routine is so insistent in its demands that it leaves little opportunity for reflection on either the past or the future.

A person's attitude to the future owes a good deal to past experience. A repeated pattern of success gives hope for future success. A long friendship or solid marriage encourages one to trust that one's spouse or friend will be faithful and supportive no matter what happens. A more or less hopeful stance in regard to the future, on the other hand, can have considerable impact on what one does in the present. An obvious example here is the way in which the realization that one has a terminal disease can radically transform all of one's attitudes. Despair about the possibility of finding a job can lead a young person to give up on his or her education. A realistic hope for professional advancement, on the other hand, can help motivate a person to be more creative and productive than ever.

Even a minimal amount of reflection soon makes it clear that there are fewer things more fundamental to our experience of life than the simple fact that we live in time, that our present comes out of and is influenced by the past and is moving toward the future. This future is something for which we are partly responsible and for which we can plan, but it is also something that in many other ways lies hidden beyond our knowledge and control.

What is true of us as individuals is also true of us as social beings. Families, institutions and organizations of various kinds, nations and churches all share the basic human situation of being in time. An organization is founded at a particular moment to serve a special purpose. Its founders commit themselves to achieve certain goals and in doing so are probably motivated by a corresponding set of ideals. The original structure reflects the perceived needs, how the founders intend to try to meet them, and the means available to do so. Time will inevitably bring change, change in the world but also in the institution itself, change in its personnel, change perhaps in the way the original goals are understood, change in the group that the institution was created to serve. Such changes demand adaptation and creativity. At certain moments in the life of many institutions the rate of change may be so intense that people are forced to go back to the beginnings in order to rediscover the founding vision and to determine whether and how in a different environment the now much-changed institution can and should continue.

Like institutions and organizations, nations and churches are also deeply marked by their past. The upheaval in Eastern Europe following the collapse of the Soviet Union bears witness to the continuing power of nationalistic and other attitudes that for decades had disappeared from the consciousness of many. Crises in nations sometimes force their citizens to go back into history in order to discover when and how certain legal and cultural patterns originated and what it was people were trying to foster or conserve in developing them.

The Catholic Church as a community of faith is known for its long and rich history. It has existed for almost two thousand years. Over that time it has entered into and interacted with a wide range of cultures. Although born in Roman Palestine, it rapidly spread throughout the countries bordering the Mediterranean and then entered into and became a part of the new culture developing in Europe. With European expansion it came to both North and South America. Over the last century or more it has spread in smaller or larger numbers to every continent and every region of the globe.

STEEPED IN HISTORY

Rome is the center of Catholic Christianity. The bishop of Rome, the pope, is regarded by Catholics as the successor to the apostle Peter and to the primacy that he exercised over the other apostles in the period of the church's beginnings. To visit Rome and especially Christian Rome is to be overwhelmed by a sense of history. Under the present St. Peter's Basilica on the Vatican hill excavations have uncovered an ancient Roman cemetery dating back to the first century and earlier. Among the mausoleums that wealthy Romans had built for themselves and their families there is a single grave that from the mid-second century at the latest became a center of pilgrimage and of religious devotion for Christians. It was there, an ancient marker affirms, that the apostle Peter was buried, probably after being martyred in the nearby forum of Nero.

When Emperor Constantine in the early fourth century granted Christianity legal status and began to support it in a variety of ways, he arranged for an impressive basilica to be constructed on Vatican hill in such a way that its altar would be directly above the site of Peter's grave. The present St. Peter's was built during the Renaissance and reflects the involvement of many of the popes of that period in the extraordinary renewal of art and culture that was then taking place. Something new was wanted and yet it had to be built to some degree on the foundations of the old. The splendor and even the hubris of the High Renaissance period and the exuberant triumphalism of the Baroque were made to serve an ancient tradition. The new forms were thought to be required by a new and expansive period in human history. The completion of the modern building coincided with the renewal of the church that marked the Catholic response to the Protestant Reformation.

To visit St. Peter's, to walk through the cemetery that still lies beneath it, to call up in one's imagination the impressive structure that Constantine's builders created, to come into the vast expanse of the present church and to marvel at Michelangelo's dome and Bernini's great baldachin over the high altar, to attend a papal Mass, to picture the immense nave of the church filled with the more than two thousand bishops who had come from all over the world to take part in Vatican II—to do this kind of thing in a reflective way is to become aware of something of the remarkable history of the Roman Catholic Church. That history is obviously not without its ambiguities. Luther's reformation was partly sparked by the preaching of an indulgence, one of the purposes of which was to raise money for the building of the new St. Peter's. But even knowing that, one cannot help but recognize and be impressed by the age and the historical experience of both the papacy and the Catholic Church.

TWO MEANINGS OF *HISTORY*

The word *history* can be used in two different ways. The first and more basic of these is very close to what is suggested by the phrase *life in time*. We are historical beings; we live in time; we live in history. Although common parlance tends to emphasize the connection of history with the past, as a dimension of life it includes past, present, and future. To have a sense of history is certainly to have a sensitivity for and awareness of the past, but it is also to be conscious of the present as rooted in and coming out of the past. It likewise involves an awareness of the future as something that to some degree grows out of the present and for which we have a responsibility.

More commonly *history* refers to a knowledge of the past. As a discipline, history made enormous strides in the course of the nineteenth century. Modeling their work to some degree on that of the natural sciences, German historians in particular struggled to develop methodologies that would enable them to give their discipline a truly scientific basis. Their ideal was to reconstruct the past "as it had really been." In spite of the considerable contribution such scholars made, their ideal has turned out to be illusory. Historical knowledge is not that clear-cut, not that precise, above all not that objective. The data with which historians work is sometimes excessively limited. As it expands and new methodologies are developed, new interpretations become necessary. In our own day significant impetus to the task of historical reconstruction has been given by asking new questions or rephrasing old ones because of a different perspective. A striking example of the former phenomenon in regard to church history has been the development of feminism and of a new and sophisticated interest in the role of women and of such issues as the influence of patriarchal cultures in Christian history. Once certain questions have been raised, everything starts to appear in a slightly different light. An example of how an old set of questions can be asked from a new perspective is found in recent studies of the Protestant Reformation. The ecumenical movement and the growing appreciation of scholars from all denominations for the faith and practice of other Christians have led to a rereading of almost everything related to Reformation history.

History is important to Catholics both as a lived reality and as an academic discipline. The church lives in time; it is rooted in the past and feels a particular loyalty and fidelity to it. At the same time its mission demands that it be in and open to the present. The church is aware of the future, both of the absolute future, which is God and the final triumph of God's kingdom, and of the more immediate future and of its responsibility to prepare for it by decisions and actions in the present.

The development of critical, historical scholarship over the last two hundred years has not been indifferent to the church and its history. In fact, over that period critical history in relation both to the Bible and to the history of the church and its teachings has become an increasingly important part of theology. In spite of certain ahistorical tendencies in contemporary culture, tendencies that put a premium on the abstract and the universal, Catholic theology continues to emphasize the importance of historical scholarship and to struggle with the ongoing challenge of the meaning of history and the place of believers in it.

HISTORY IN THE CREED AND IN THE LITURGY

One of the more surprising things about the Christian creed is its mention of a relatively minor Roman administrative official, Pontius Pilate. Someone coming upon the creed as a statement of Christian faith for the first time might well ask why his name should be included in it alongside its affirmations about the Father, the Son, and the Spirit as creator, redeemer, and sanctifier respectively. Much of the creed confesses fundamental and in some sense universal religious truths. These are about God and about what God has done and continues to do for us. Pilate is someone who, had it not been for the creed, would be all but unknown today. That he is known is due in no small measure to the importance that Christian faith gives to history.

The mention of Pilate anchors faith in Jesus Christ in a particular time and place. Christians do not simply believe in the idea of a Messiah or of a God-man, but rather in a specific historical figure, the first-century Palestinian Jew Jesus of Nazareth; he is the one in whom God entered in a new and definitive way into human history and in doing so renewed it from within. The idea of the divine and the human coming together, the idea of the incarnation, is central to Christianity. More important than the idea, however, is the faith assertion that in Jesus God in fact did become incarnate. It is the historical reality of Jesus and therefore of Christian origins that the appearance of Pilate in the creed underlines.

Christianity is a historical religion, not just in the sense that, like all things human, it exists in history or that it began at a particular moment of history, but rather because it believes that history itself is the medium in and through which God comes to us. What is true of Christ, we said in the first chapter, is often true of his body as well. The church has not only a historical origin but a historical destiny. Its mission is tied up with the whole sweep of human history; with and in it, the church too is moving toward fulfillment in God.

What is suggested by the creed is reinforced in the liturgy and especially in the eucharist, the heart and soul of the church's life of prayer and worship. In celebrating the eucharist believers make memory of the life, teaching, and destiny of Jesus. In doing so they see themselves as fulfilling an explicit command that Jesus formulated at the last supper: "Do this in memory of me." The Greek word here for memory is *anamnesis*. Its biblical background suggests that it means something more than mere remembering. Even as the liturgy recalls what Jesus said and did, and especially his death and resurrection, it cries out to God for an outpouring of the Spirit. It is the Spirit who renders present among us the saving reality of which we make memory. The barrier between past and present is broken through and the once and for all event of Christ's sacrifice touches us with its transformative power.

The eucharist—and indeed the whole of the liturgy—looks to and remembers the past in order to bring about present change and to turn us in creative and active ways toward the future. It looks forward to our fulfillment and the fulfillment of the world in God at the end of time. It challenges and enables us to live here and now in ways that will bring our world one step closer to that fulfillment.

CREATOR AND LORD OF HISTORY

What the creed affirms and what the liturgy celebrates and renders present are rooted in the faith and experience of Israel. The Bible in its present form begins with the story of creation. The two versions of the story, contained in the first three chapters of Genesis, affirm in simple but poetic language a number of fundamental truths of biblical religion. Everything that is depends for its being on God. God transcends all that we can see or measure; indeed God transcends everything that we can know. At the same time the transcendent God is the source of all that is. Because all things come from God, they are in their fundamental being radically good. Human beings have a special place in God's creation. They are made in the divine image and likeness; they are called to live in God's presence and to exercise care and responsibility for one another and for the world. Unfortunately, this is not the whole of the human story. Humans are endowed with freedom and are able to turn away from God and to make themselves the center of their concerns and hopes. The second great lesson that the Book of Genesis teaches about humanity—after what it says about human dignity—is that we are capable of sin and self-destructiveness and that such things have become a part of human history.

According to the Bible, God did not abandon humankind to its own fate but continued in various ways to be present to human history and to offer people a way of salvation. The manner in which the story of Noah and its aftermath are presented suggests that we are to interpret the flood as a new creation and a new beginning. God establishes a covenant with Noah and his descendants and promises that the earth will never suffer such devastation again. God's involvement takes on a new form with Abraham and Sarah and with their children and their children's children. God's historical activity becomes more focused, tending toward the creation of a people who will become in a new way God's partners in working out the divine plan for human salvation.

Israel discovered both its God and its own identity in one and the same event, the event of the exodus. The one who revealed himself to them as their God is a God of salvation, a God who hears and responds to the cry of the poor, a God of people, a God who remains present to the life of those whom he calls into a special relationship.

Perhaps the most remarkable single text in the Hebrew scriptures is the account in the Book of Exodus of the vocation of Moses. In spite of the unusual circumstances of his birth, the young Moses knows himself to be an Israelite. When the story opens he is tending the flock of his father-in-law in the desert of Sinai. A theophany or revelation of God takes place in the form of a burning bush. God reveals himself as the God of Abraham and Isaac and Jacob; God announces his intention to send Moses to lead the Hebrews out of their slavery and suffering in Egypt. Moses asks God to reveal his name so that he will have something to say to those who ask him on whose authority he has come to them. "God said to Moses, '*I am who I am.*' He said further, 'Thus you shall say to the Israelites: *I am* has sent me to you'" (Ex 3:14).

The precise meaning of God's name is not immediately clear. Some have even wondered whether what God is quoted as saying is not perhaps a refusal to reveal the divine name at all. They understand the phrase to be saying something like: "I am who I am, and I have no intention of revealing my name to you." This hardly seems likely, given the special devotion with which Jews have always regarded this passage and the name Yahweh that is rooted in it. Like the name given in the text quoted above, *Yahweh* too comes from the Hebrew verb "to be" and probably means "the one who is."

The Hebrew verb form used in the phrase *"I am who I am"* suggests action. God seems to be revealed here as someone who will be involved in Israel's ongoing life. One possible translation is, "I will be with you, as who I am I will be with you." God's name is a promise, a promise of God's active presence in the midst of the people. God will be with them and go before them on their historical journey.

In the Bible God is both the creator and the lord of history—a God who cares, a God who out of love becomes involved in human history and in the life of a particular people with whom God makes a covenant. A great deal of the Bible is the story of that covenant. It takes the form of history, an account of Israel's history and its successes and failures. The prophets help their compatriots to discern in their history what God is doing and what God is asking of them at a given moment. Like so much of the Bible, the books of the prophets talk a great deal about history. They recall the past and especially the marvelous deeds that God did on behalf of Israel at the time of the exodus. They also talk a good deal about the present and about the meaning in God's eyes of current events. They evoke the future either as a warning to the people to change their ways or as a promise that God will soon come and save them from their suffering.

From a biblical perspective, religion and history are inseparable. If, as we saw in chapter 1, the focus of the Bible is more on the community than on individuals, that community is clearly a historical community. It is in history that it first encountered its God, and it is through all the concrete and disparate elements and moments of its historical existence that it tries to respond to God. The God who was manifested as a God of salvation in the origins of the people will bring them and all of human history to fulfillment at the end of time.

JESUS AND THE END OF TIME

Mark sums up the basic content of the preaching of Jesus in what at first sight seems to be a remarkably simple sentence: "The time is fulfilled and the kingdom of God has come near; repent, and believe in the good news" (Mk 1:15). The faith and history of Israel provide a necessary background for understanding what Jesus is saying here. A new moment in history is dawning—"the time is fulfilled." A period of time that had first to pass has passed, and now God is about to do a new thing. The language about the coming of the kingdom suggests that the new moment is not just one more stage in God's plan of salvation but its definitive fulfillment. Although the hopes of Israel were many sided and although they found a variety of forms in the time of Jesus, there was a sense that the coming of the kingdom would entail the final triumph of God and God's ways and would usher in the end of history as we know it.

Everything that Jesus said and did has to be seen in relation to his preaching of the kingdom. There seems to be no doubt that his teaching and activity raised considerable expectations among those who heard and saw him. The consensus was that the definitive coming of God's kingdom would transform history as it had been experienced up until then. It would bring forgiveness and healing and the triumph of good over evil. Some hoped that it would involve the overthrow of the Roman occupation and the reestablishment of Israel as a free and independent nation.

The rejection and death of Jesus cast a pall of despair over his followers. The two disciples on the road to Emmaus, in explaining to the mysterious stranger who accompanied them what Jesus had meant to them, put it this way: "We had hoped that he was the one to redeem Israel" (Lk 24:21). As much as the cross, however, seemed to give the lie to the claims implicit in Jesus' life and activity, the experience of the resurrection—the conviction that God had raised Jesus from the dead and had manifested him to Mary Magdalen, Peter, and the others—validated them. God was with him, with him even unto and beyond death. God's raising of Jesus to the fullness of life as well as the death through which he had passed came to be regarded as saving events; they represent a new and definitive act on behalf of humanity on the part of the God of salvation. The paschal mystery, the mystery of the death and resurrection of Jesus, constitutes a new exodus; it seals a new and universal covenant. The outpouring of the Spirit of the risen Christ on Pentecost was interpreted by Peter as a fulfillment of a prophecy of Joel for the end times (cf. Acts 2:14–24). There was a widespread sense among believers that the end was near. The earliest extant Christian writing, the first letter of Paul to the Thessalonians, deals with concerns that have arisen because some of the members of that community have already died. Paul's insistence on the proximity of the return of Christ made them wonder about the fate of believers who might die before he comes. Paul assures them "that we who are alive, who are left until the coming of the Lord, will by no means precede those who have died." When Christ comes, "the dead in Christ will rise first. Then we who are alive, who are left, will be caught up in the clouds together with them to meet the Lord in the air; and so we will be with the Lord forever" (1 Thes 4:15–18).

The imagery of this text reflects Paul's Jewish background. What is important for our purposes is the insight it gives that for many of the first Christians the event of the death and resurrection of Jesus was perceived to be of such significance that it could only be understood as the prelude to the end of history and to the final establishment of God's kingdom.

The Greek word for the end is *eschaton*. It has given birth to the somewhat technical but helpful English terms *eschatology* and *eschatological*. Both words refer to the end times. In the context of first-century Jewish hopes, the mention of the near approach of the kingdom of God in the preaching of Jesus could not help but awaken "eschatological" expectations. Such expectations were reinforced by the experience of the resurrection. Those Jews who believed in a resurrection of the dead associated it with the end of history and with the definitive establishment of God's kingdom.

As time passed and the hoped-for return of Christ continued to be delayed, Christians had to rethink their understanding of the meaning of what had happened. That something definitive had taken place in and through the life and destiny of Jesus was certain. Their conviction in this regard was reinforced by their experience of the gift of the Spirit. The paschal mystery and the life of Jesus of which it was the climax came to be seen as inaugurating a new and final stage in human history. If the end in the sense of the definitive establishment of God's kingdom had not yet come, in another sense believers were already living in the end times. The death and resurrection of Jesus marked a turning point. "In Christ God was reconciling the world to himself" (2 Cor 5:19). Christ Jesus "was handed over to death for our trespasses and was raised for our justification" (Rom 4:25). The gospel about the death and resurrection of Jesus "is the power of God for salvation to everyone who has faith, to the Jew first and also to the Greek" (Rom 1:16).

The first believers lived in a kind of eschatological tension. When they came together they prayed "*Maranatha,* come, Lord Jesus, come." At the same time they rejoiced in what had already taken place: the forgiveness and justification that was theirs through faith in the paschal mystery and through the outpouring of the Spirit. The latter was thought of as the first fruits of the fulfillment that still awaited them in the future. People recognized with increasing clarity that a new epoch of human history had begun. They thought of it as the time of the Spirit, the time of the church.

The church as the community of believers was there from the beginning. Foreshadowed by the group of disciples that gathered around Jesus, it was established in a more definitive way with the coming of the Spirit at Pentecost and with the preaching of Peter. The apostolic witness and the gift of the Spirit drew believers into community with one another and related them both to the historical Jesus and to the risen Christ, whose body they now formed. With the passage of time and especially with the death of the apostles and of the first generation of believers, a concerted effort was made to give the church the forms and structures and the self-understanding that would enable it not only to survive in history but to fulfill its historic mission.

THE TIME OF THE CHURCH

The gospel of Luke and the Acts of the Apostles are often viewed as two volumes of a single work. The first tells the story of Jesus and the second that of the early church. The gospel begins and ends in the Temple of Jerusalem, the center of Jewish ritual and religious life. Acts also begins in Jerusalem with the ascension and the coming of the Spirit at Pentecost. Subsequent chapters recount the expansion of the church through Judea and Samaria and out into the world of the eastern Mediterranean. The book ends with St. Paul, under house arrest in Rome, "proclaiming the kingdom of God and teaching about the Lord Jesus Christ with all boldness and without hindrance" to all who came to him (Acts 28:31). This scene, with Paul in the capital of the great empire of the day preaching the gospel, symbolizes for Luke the dramatic growth in self-awareness and missionary outreach that marked the early decades of the church's life. Having now reached the heart of the pagan empire, it is resolutely embarked on its historic destiny as a church of Gentiles as well as of Jews.

Luke informs his readers in the opening verses of his gospel that he has undertaken "to set down an orderly account of the events that have been fulfilled among us," and in order to do so he has collated the material "handed on to us by those who from the beginning were eyewitnesses and servants of the word" (Lk 1:1–3). Near the beginning of Acts he tells of the need the first disciples felt to find a replacement for Judas among the twelve. It is clear from both documents that for Luke the apostles are to play a crucial role in the ongoing life of the church. Unlike Paul, he tends to identify the apostles, at least in the strong sense of that word, with the twelve. They are those who were with Jesus from the beginning of his public ministry and who were also witnesses to the resurrection. Their testimony forms a connecting link between the life of Jesus and the life of the church. To use an image that becomes explicit in Ephesians, they, with the prophets, are the foundation on which the church is built, "with Christ Jesus himself as the cornerstone" (Eph 2:20).

Some of the later books of the New Testament, like the Acts of the Apostles, 1 Peter, and the so-called pastoral letters, those to Timothy and Titus, reflect a growing preoccupation with church structures and with the content of faith. Church leaders are encouraged to "guard the good treasure," to "hold to the standard of sound teaching that you have heard from me" (2 Tm 1:13–14), to protect their flock from the ravages of heresy and division. Paul is portrayed in Acts and in the pastoral letters as ensuring a kind of succession in his responsibility of church leadership. The concern in these writings with historical continuity in regard both to the content of the faith and to the form of church leadership has led some Protestant scholars to see in them and in other books of the New Testament a manifestation of what they call "early Catholicism."

What one can discover in the New Testament in its initial form becomes much more evident in the course of the second century. From its beginnings Christianity was faced with enormous challenges, some coming from without and some from within. The creativity and decision making that such challenges provoked helped the community to clarify and give formal expression to some of its most typically Catholic features.

The major theological and religious challenge that confronted the early church came from a widespread but somewhat amorphous religious movement known as Gnosticism. The term comes from the Greek word *gnosis* or "knowledge." The movement was highly syncretistic and could be found in Jewish and pagan as well as Christian forms. Marked by an exuberance of mythological imagery and a rich variety of religious-philosophical speculation, it reflected at its deepest level a profound pessimism about the material world, the human body, and the meaning of history. Christian Gnostics opposed the Old and the New Testaments. They held that the Father of Jesus Christ is not the creator God. The former dwells in a purely spiritual realm unrelated to the material world. The God of creation is a lesser God whose creative activity was the result of some fundamental flaw in the heavenly world. Some human beings are more favored than others. They have in them a spark of the higher, spiritual world. It was to reveal to them their true identity that the Christ has come down from above. The incarnation was not real, or if it was, the heavenly Son departed before the crucifixion. Salvation is not by faith in Christ or by a moral response to the gift of the Spirit, but by knowledge alone.

Confronted by Catholic bishops and theologians who argued that such ideas had little in common with the New Testament and the traditional teaching of the churches, the Gnostics countered by claiming that they had a succession of teachers that reached back to the apostles; from them they had learned those deeper truths of religion that ordinary believers are incapable of receiving. They appealed to texts like the one in the letter to the Hebrews that distinguishes between the "milk" of doctrine that is given to infants in the faith and "solid food, (which) is for the mature, for those whose faculties have been trained by practice to distinguish good from evil" (Heb 5:13–14). The Gnostics claimed that they were offering people the kind of substantial food that only the truly spiritual person can digest.

In defending the creed of the church against such theories, theologians like Irenaeus and Tertullian took a double tack. In regard to the content of faith they emphasized the continuity that exists between the Old and the New Testaments, between creation and redemption in Christ. The God of Israel is the Father of Jesus Christ. There is no other God. The body and the material world, no matter how powerfully sin has touched them, remain part of God's creation and as such are fundamentally good. Salvation is not simply of souls but of human beings. The flesh, Tertullian insisted, is the key to salvation. Christ died in the flesh for us. It is through the materiality of the sacramental economy that we are brought into contact with his saving grace. Christian hope is not simply about the immortality of the soul but about the resurrection of the body and about a new heaven and a new earth. As seductive as the Gnostic vision was, church leaders refused to succumb to any form of radical dualism, whether between flesh and spirit, creation and God, or the Old and the New Testaments.

In response to the Gnostic claims to a secret succession of teachers, the same theologians pointed to the history of various churches and to the lists kept in them of their bishops. In some cases these reached back to the time of Christian origins. It is the bishops, they argued, who are the public and official teachers of Christian truth; they have been installed in the chair *(cathedra)* of the apostles. The fact of apostolic succession together with the gift of the Spirit that is theirs through ordination give their teaching a special kind of authority.

In this and other second-century debates two themes that have remained central to Catholic identity came to the fore. These are apostolic succession and apostolic tradition. Although the two realities are closely related, the more basic of them is apostolic tradition. This phrase points to the conviction that the faith of the church goes back to, and is fundamentally the same as, the faith of the apostles. The Latin root of the word *tradition* suggests a handing on or a handing over of something to someone. In the present context it refers both to a process and to a content. The teaching of the apostles has been handed down to subsequent generations in their writings but also in the life and liturgy, the creeds and common convictions of the various churches. Apostolic succession refers in a special way to the role of bishops in regard to this process and to the fact that one can trace back their lineage through local church lists to the apostolic generation. Second-century writers attributed special importance to those churches they believed were founded by the apostles, churches like those at Ephesus and Corinth and especially Rome, which they regarded as being built on the teaching and martyrdom of both Peter and Paul. The consensus was that apostolic succession existed in order to protect, serve, and hand on apostolic tradition.

Second-century struggles thus strengthened the Catholic sense of the role of bishops and of tradition. The apostolic witness provides a firm foundation that the church can neither dilute nor abandon. A concern for apostolicity is a concern that the present faith and practice of the church should be in continuity with the life and teaching of the apostles. It remains a central concern of Catholicism. The office of bishop is meant to serve the church's apostolicity every bit as much as its unity.

THE CHURCH IN HISTORY;
THE HISTORY OF THE CHURCH

The emphasis in the early church on apostolicity, in terms of continuity with the past, and on an almost static understanding of the process of tradition contains a paradox. At the very time that Catholic bishops and theologians were insisting on the traditional nature of the church's faith and practice, these were undergoing a very real although subtle process of development and adaptation. In its origins Christianity was fundamentally a Jewish phenomenon. Not only was Jesus a Jew, but the earliest expressions of Christian faith were almost entirely formulated in Jewish language and categories. Jesus was the Messiah, the Christ, of Israel. His ministry was understood in terms of the coming of the kingdom of God. The Our Father, the prayer that Jesus himself taught his followers, could hardly have been more Jewish. The eucharist not only goes back to various Jewish ritual meals, but the great prayer of praise and thanksgiving that came to determine its structure has obvious Jewish parallels.

As profoundly Jewish as Christianity initially was, by the end of the second century it was becoming more and more at home in the predominantly Hellenistic culture of the Mediterranean world. With remarkable openness and creativity thinkers like Justin and Origen entered into dialogue with Greek and Roman cultures and especially with philosophy. The process was not an easy one, nor did everyone agree on the wisdom of some of the things that were said and done. Some churches and individuals were in fact more open to Hellenism than others. Clement of Alexandria, for example, thought of Plato as a forerunner of Christ and of philosophy in general as functioning among the Greeks in a manner analogous to the way the Mosaic law did for Jews. Tertullian of Carthage, on the other hand, was convinced that philosophy is the root of all heresy. What is there in common, he asked, between Jerusalem and Athens? In spite of such differences, Christianity by the third century had entered into a positive and enriching relationship with elements of classical culture, a relationship that became a key factor in the heritage that the patristic period left to medieval Catholicism.

Some scholars have maintained that the "Hellenization of Christianity" entailed a dilution if not a loss of Christian substance. Others have denied the charge and argued that what went forward in the early church reveals a law of Catholic life. Concern for tradition and for maintaining the purity of the gospel went hand in hand with an awareness of the need to relate the Christian message to different cultural situations. This was seen as a necessary precondition for it to be understood and accepted by people living within various cultures. In this sense some form of Hellenization was essential for the continuing vitality of the church and for the success of its missionary activity. In the fourth and fifth centuries a series of remarkable bishops and theologians, including Augustine in the West, helped to create what is regarded by many as a high point in Catholic history by their appropriation for Christian faith of much that was best in late classical culture.

Lack of space prohibits us from dealing at any length with the subsequent history of the church. A study of that history, however, would reveal how the double concern of continuity with the past and openness to the present have remained key principles in the development of Catholicism. At different times one or the other of these concerns tended to be paramount in people's minds. Until the modern period and its development of critical historical scholarship there was sometimes a blindness to the fact of development and certainly to its extent. From the beginning of the nineteenth century an increasing number of Catholics became sensitive to the centrality of development to Catholic history and Catholic identity. The most famous English language treatment of the theme in the last century was John Henry Newman's *Essay on the Development of Christian Doctrine.* As a historian Newman recognized the differences that existed between the faith and practice of the church in the medieval and the patristic periods. As an Anglican he was inclined to see the later forms as a falling away from an original purity. Further reflection led him to the conviction that they represented not a false but a true development. Vatican II, in building on his ideas and those of others, recognized in the process of development a traditional feature of the way the church appropriates God's revelation in Christ in changing circumstances.

Another phenomenon that a history of Catholicism would reveal is the seriousness with which bishops and theologians over the centuries have struggled with the meaning of history and with the place of the church in it. Although the movement away from Christianity's biblical roots resulted in some people being less sensitive to the importance of history for faith and to the historical mission of the church, again and again one encounters thinkers and church leaders who turned to the history of Israel for patterns and examples that they could use to illuminate their own times. The ups and downs of the relationship between the church and the political order suggested obvious parallels with the history of Israel. Bishops and popes in confronting kings and emperors saw themselves fulfilling the classic role of prophets. Medieval Christendom with its interweaving of priesthood and empire seems in many ways to have been modeled on biblical experience. Heresies and schisms among Christians evoked the tragic division that marked the relationship between the northern and southern parts of the Jewish kingdom. Persecuted churches related their experiences to that of the Israelites in Egypt or of the people during the Babylonian exile. In the mirror of such incidents believers found hope and courage in confronting the trials and difficulties they had to face.

VATICAN II AND THE IMPORTANCE OF HISTORY

In the *Pastoral Constitution on the Church in the Modern World*, Vatican II comments on the shift that has taken place in the course of the twentieth century in the consciousness that many people have of the world and of their place in it. They have substituted "a dynamic and more evolutionary concept of nature for a static one" (no. 5). Their sense of the pace of historical change has quickened. So also has their awareness of their responsibility for being actively involved in it. In regard to the relation of the church and culture, the same document recognizes the positive significance of past encounters of Christianity with different cultures and affirms that "this kind of adaptation and preaching of the revealed Word must ever be the law of all evangelization" (no. 44). The new emphasis on history and on the importance and the need of the church to discern the challenges and possibilities that God as the Lord of history is opening up for humanity and for the church in it led the bishops to insist on the significance of what they called "the signs of the time."

John XXIII had already used the phrase in his 1963 encyclical *Pacem in terris (Peace on Earth)*. It reflects a heightened sense of the historical dimension of life. Economic, social, political, and other realities change. Such changes often create new problems, suggest new ways of doing things, challenge old values, force people to deal with new needs. The church sees itself in solidarity with all of humanity and especially with those who are most in need. As the *Pastoral Constitution on the Church in the Modern World* put it: "The joy and hope, the grief and the anguish of the people of our time, especially of those who are poor or afflicted in any way, are the joy and hope, the grief and anguish of the followers of Christ as well. Nothing that is genuinely human fails to find an echo in their hearts" (no. 1). It is not enough simply to affirm the eternal truths of the gospel. They need to be brought into a vital relationship with the concrete situations within which people are actually living. The attempt to understand their situations and to discover how concretely the Christian conscience is being challenged by them is at the heart of what is involved in discerning the signs of the time. Such discernment is the necessary precondition for any significant involvement in overcoming endemic injustice and oppression. Catholic social doctrine requires this kind of discernment if it is to make any real difference to those whom it is most intended to help.

The theme of history comes back in a number of other areas of Vatican II as well. As indicated in chapter 1, the image of the church to which the council gives the greatest emphasis is the image of the people of God. Among the many theological themes that this image brings out is that of history. The people of the Bible are often presented as a pilgrim people, a people on a journey, not yet at its final destination. This was particularly true of the time of the exodus and of the forty years in the desert. It was given a new meaning during the period of the exile. The letter to the Hebrews picks up the same image and applies it to the church. It, too, is a pilgrim people, caught up on a journey and not yet at its final resting place in God (Heb 4:1–11).

The image of a pilgrim people, while not by itself capable of bringing out all aspects of the life and mission of the church, does underline its historical nature and destiny. The church is like a people on a journey. As much as it has its identity from Christ, it lives in history; its journey brings it into contact with various peoples and cultures. It undergoes temptations and struggles and adapts itself to changing intellectual and social climates. Change and adaptation, growth and development, are of the essence of the church's life. Such things flow inevitably from its fundamentally historical nature. Nor are they the mere result of the historical character of all human institutions. The church is called both to live in history and to take history seriously; it is a people and therefore a human community, but more important, it is the people of God, the people of a God who in the story of Israel and of Jesus is revealed as the Lord of history. God is present to human history and present in a special way to the historical pilgrimage of the church.

The church is neither static nor perfect. Living in history, it is part of a dynamic and changing process. Because of its faith in a God who has promised to be actively present with the people, it lives in hope for God's help and for future fulfillment. Vatican II brought back to the consciousness of many Catholics a sense of the eschatological nature of the church. As much as present failures and inadequacies may depress us, we look forward to personal and ecclesial fulfillment with the final coming of Christ and his kingdom at the end of history.

CONFLICT ABOUT HISTORY

To have even a cursory awareness of church history is to know that it has often been marked by conflict and tension. Decisions of real historical import are rarely clear-cut or easy. Equally sincere and intelligent people can come to very different practical judgments about what should or should not be done in a particular situation. This was already the case in the early church in regard to whether Gentile converts to Christianity should be required to follow the Mosaic law or not. Paul's view on this eventually carried the day but not without serious disagreement and even confrontation. The work of the first several ecumenical councils and the writing of the creeds were fraught with enormous difficulty and provoked deep and bitter divisions. Outsiders sometimes marvel and even scoff at the passion that went into what seem to have been very small differences. To those involved in the debates, however, the truth of the gospel was at stake.

Vatican II has clearly been the most important event in relation to the institutional life of the church in the twentieth century. Even before it was over, its teaching had become a focus of conflict. Some felt that in a number of ways it had not gone far enough. Others believed that it had gone too far. In fact, the debate about the texts was only the beginning. They called for things to be done and actions to be taken across a wide range of areas including liturgy, ecumenism, religious life, the education of seminarians, the involvement of lay people in the life and mission of the church, and the presence and activity of the church in the modern world. As the church as a whole and as various groups within it began to respond to the directives of the council in these different areas, debates intensified and sometimes became acrimonious. In some countries this resulted in a rather vociferous polarization of positions. Although many individual issues were involved, increasingly the divisions turned around the council itself and its historic significance. Did it represent a radically new moment in the history of the church, or should its continuity with what went before be stressed? One reason for the polarization was the failure to develop a commonly shared view of how Vatican II fit into the broader history of the church, how it related, for example, to European Christendom, to the Protestant Reformation, and to the long struggle with the heritage of the Enlightenment and of the French and American revolutions. A serious effort to situate the council in relation to these and other important moments in church history would have helped people to see the genuine novelty that it represented but also to appreciate its profound continuity with the Catholic past.

The post-conciliar period has witnessed a number of conflicts in which the meaning of history has played a critical role. Liberation theology, a particularly striking example, grew out of a deepening awareness on the part of church leaders in Latin America of the kind of social and other changes that were taking place in the world and which were reflected in Vatican II's *Pastoral Constitution on the Church in the Modern World.* There was a sense that the church had been too passive in the face of economic and other forms of injustice. People were often helped to cope with and to survive in unjust situations rather than encouraged to change them. Liberation theologians appealed to the Hebrew scriptures and to the experience of the Israelites. They too had been an oppressed people and had encountered God in the process of their liberation out of slavery. The prophets confronted the rich and the powerful of their day and took the side of the poor and the dispossessed. Jesus' preaching of the kingdom of God, the same theologians argued, cannot be restricted to a personal and purely spiritual salvation. The God of redemption is the God of creation. Salvation includes a process of helping humanity to become what God intended it to be from the beginning.

Biblical arguments like these were brought into relationship with modern philosophical and sociological theories about history and the role that human beings are called to play in giving it direction to create a theology that challenged the status quo. Its opponents accused it of Marxism and of reducing the gospel to its social implications. Whatever the exaggerations of particular individuals, liberation theology clearly has helped to bring back to Catholic consciousness something that is central to Christian faith: our relationship to God is inseparable from our attitude to and involvement in history. The coming of Jesus did not end history but rather inaugurated a new period in it. The sermon on the mount and the double commandment of love of God and love of neighbor have implications for life in the world. The church of Christ must be marked by a preferential love or option for the poor. Faith is not meant to draw people out of history but to motivate and empower them to take responsibility for it and to become active agents in its transformation.

The issue of history is central to the debate about the ordination of women. The major reason the leadership of the Catholic Church believes itself unable to ordain women, according to a 1976 document of the Vatican Congregation for the Doctrine of the Faith, is that it is against the tradition of the church. The document appeals to the fact that Jesus himself, while open to and supportive of women in ways that went beyond the expectations of his time, did not include them among the twelve. The Congregation sees the practice of Jesus continued and reaffirmed in the fact that women were not ordained as priests or bishops by the apostles or by their successors. The unbroken nature of the tradition from the time of Jesus to the present is seen as a sign that it is God's will that only males should be ordained to the priesthood. The document goes on to offer a secondary theological argument to suggest why this is the case. It deals with the way, in the sacramental order, the priest is required to act "in the person of Christ." It is said that the fullness of the symbolism involved in such activity would be undermined by having women act "in the person" of the male Christ. The longstanding character of the traditional practice and its recent solemn reaffirmation by John Paul II has led Cardinal Ratzinger, the prefect of the Congregation of the Doctrine of the Faith, to publish a letter stating his conviction that the traditional teaching represents an act of the ordinary magisterium of the church and is to be considered infallible.

The topic raises a host of issues and has provoked a considerable number of publications. An important feature of the debate for our purpose is the varying approaches to history that it reveals. Those who argue against the ordination of women appeal to a traditional practice that they say cannot be changed. Those who for various reasons believe that ordination should be open to women recall the phenomenon of development. Tradition, in the Catholic understanding, is not a static but rather a dynamic and developing reality that is able to adapt itself to a variety of contexts and situations. Central here, as elsewhere, is the role of the Spirit. The Spirit is a principle of life and newness in the church as well as of fidelity to the truth of the gospel. In this debate, as in so many others, people of good will find themselves on different sides. Only continuing history and a prayerful and intelligent openness to the signs of the times and to what the Spirit is saying to the church through them will overcome the impasse.

CATHOLICISM AND HISTORY

In spite of a certain prejudice in elements of North American society against it, history as an academic discipline and as knowledge of the past remains an important element of modern culture and a key instrument for understanding contemporary life, whether individual or communal. It is particularly helpful for coming to any balanced appreciation of the Catholic Church. It would be difficult to think of any organization or institution in Western culture that has a longer or richer history behind it. Nor is that history simply part of the past. The church lives in history, and much of its present identity is the result of creative reactions to the challenges and possibilities it has encountered in the course of it. Let one example stand for many: the papacy and its institutions—and the way that they relate to the world and the church—are incomprehensible apart from an appreciation of their history.

More than being a historical institution, the Catholic Church takes history seriously from the point of view of its faith. The God of biblical religion is the Lord of history. Far from being distant from and indifferent to the human condition, God was revealed in the experience of Israel as a God of salvation and a God of people. God cares about and is involved with human beings in their search for wholeness and meaning. This is the God whose kingdom Jesus preached and whom he addressed as Abba, Father. The incarnation of the divine Word in Jesus of Nazareth led to the establishment of a new and universal covenant in which all peoples were invited to share. God remains involved in our history just as God was and is involved in the history of the people of the Mosaic covenant.

The kingdom of God is among us. It exists in a special way when justice is done, peace established, and God's name is recognized and blessed. The church exists to bear witness to this kingdom, to serve it, to foster its final coming. At the same time Christians know that the fulfillment of the kingdom still lies ahead. The church is as much turned to the future as to the past. Rooted in the once and for all event of the life and destiny of Jesus and animated and guided in its present struggles by the inspiration of the Spirit, it looks forward in hope to final salvation beyond time in God's eternity.

The sense of living between past and future marks almost every aspect of the church's life. It is, for example, a key to its liturgy. It is also central to many of the most difficult issues that the church currently faces. Church leaders feel a particular responsibility for the revelation and grace given us in Christ. The notions of apostolic tradition and apostolic succession emphasize the bond they are called to maintain with the teaching of the apostles. At the same time they have a responsibility to lead the church into the future. The Spirit of Christ is still with the church, still inspiring its various members to respond to the challenges and possibilities that ongoing history continues to open up. How the church is to do this in individual cases is not always obvious. Here is a source of conflict and tension. Everyone in the church is not endowed with the same gifts and sensitivities; everyone is not entrusted with the same responsibilities. What is needed is a Catholic openness of people to one another so that the voice of the Spirit will be truly heard.

The year 2000 seems to be provoking a variety of reactions in the minds and hearts of people. Some view it with a certain fear. John Paul II encourages us to see it as a time of celebration, thanksgiving, and renewal. In Jesus, God entered our history in order to heal it and to make it an instrument of salvation. The coming of the millennium is an opportunity for believers to think about history, about its importance to us as people of faith, about the fact, too, that it is moving, however mysteriously, toward its fulfillment. It invites us with a special intensity to reflect on the ways in which we are contributing, positively or negatively to that process. Just as love of God and love of neighbor are inseparable, so too are worship of God and care for God's creation and for the continuing history of all God's people.

BELONGING TO A HISTORICAL COMMUNITY

If becoming or being a Catholic involves an invitation to leave behind loneliness and isolation and to enter into a genuine community of faith, this chapter has tried to bring out that that community is much larger than the local parish or diocese or even the universal church of our time. For me personally, one of the most enriching and consoling aspects of being a Catholic has been the sense of community that I have come to feel with the whole of the Catholic tradition, with the countless women and men who over the centuries have lived their human and Christian lives within the church and have endowed it with their spiritual, moral, artistic, and intellectual gifts. There is something wonderful about a group of Catholics chanting the litany of the saints. We are the heirs of John and Paul, of Athanasius and John Chrysostom, of Ambrose and Gregory the Great, of Benedict and Francis, of Catherine of Siena and Teresa of Avila, of all those people who in the distant and not so distant past have enriched our common heritage by their extraordinary gifts and dedication. My own understanding of Catholicism owes an enormous amount to people such as Augustine and Thomas Aquinas and John Henry Newman, not to mention Catholic theologians and writers of a more recent vintage.

The contemporary Catholic Church faces many difficulties. Some come from without, some from within. We are all disheartened by stories of priests and religious who have not only failed to live up to their vows but have caused real harm to the very people they were meant to serve. Sometimes we are disturbed by what we see as failures of church leaders to respond to changing cultural situations as rapidly as we think they should. History can help us deal with all such phenomena. The church has never been perfect. Its life has been marked by sin and failure as well as by growth and great holiness. As a historical community, we are still very much on the way to God's fullness. That thought can help us cope with our inadequacies even as it challenges us to renewal and greater dedication.

CHAPTER THREE

A Community of Faith

North American Catholics, living as they do in a multiethnic and largely secular environment, are increasingly conscious that what binds them together more than anything else is a common faith. They may disagree on occasion about the precise contours of their faith or about how it can most effectively be formulated today, but they recognize its fundamental significance for their identity.

That having faith is important to Christianity is an affirmation that most Christians, even those living more or less on the edge of church life, would be willing to admit. Differences, however, arise as soon as people attempt to articulate more precisely what they understand by *faith*. For some, the word does little more than suggest a basically religious stance in regard to life. Life has meaning and this meaning is rooted in something or someone other and greater than the world of phenomena. In the more extreme cases, the experiential or subjective element of faith is so one-sidedly stressed that the question whether or not it corresponds to something objective is thought irrelevant. This is the type of phenomenon to which a popular form of literature refers when it says that people need faith of some kind in order to cope with life.

Such a narrowly subjective understanding of faith has nothing to do with traditional Christianity. Faith there is clearly faith in God and in Christ and in the saving significance of his death and resurrection. Faith in this context is a response to a prior act of God. God becomes involved in human history and in doing so reveals something of the divine nature and of the divine will for humanity. Faith involves an acceptance of revelation and a willingness to commit ourselves to God and then to the life to which God calls us.

BIBLICAL FAITH

The Christian experience and understanding of faith is rooted in and built on the religious experience of Israel. The old Roman canon of the Mass or, as it is now called, the first eucharistic prayer, refers to Abraham as our father in faith. The phrase is meant not only to recall the historical continuity that exists between Judaism and Christianity but to underline the fact that Abraham offers in his life a model or pattern of what authentic biblical faith entails. Those who introduced the reference to Abraham into the eucharistic liturgy were probably inspired to do so by the example of Paul and of the letter to the Hebrews. In his letter to the Romans, Paul points to Abraham as a biblical example of someone who was justified not by works but by faith (Rom 4:1–25). Chapter 11 of Hebrews offers an overview of biblical history in terms of the faith of its principal characters. Abraham looms large in its presentation:

> By faith Abraham obeyed when he was called to set out for a place that he was to receive as an inheritance; and he set out, not knowing where he was going.... By faith Abraham, when put to the test, offered up Isaac. He who had received the promise was ready to offer up his only son.... He considered the fact that God is able even to raise someone from the dead—and figuratively speaking, he did receive him back. (Heb 11:8–19)

The word *faith* in the Hebrew scriptures evokes a person's fundamental response to the God who has become involved in and who is revealed by events in history. God calls Abraham not to enter a monastery or to embark on some particular form of a disciplined religious life but to set out on a journey, to leave his home and his people for a land that he does not know. God promises to be with him and, more than that, promises that Abraham and Sarah, in spite of their age, will become the ancestors of a great people. They believe what God has said, entrust themselves to God's promise, and accept the risk of the unknown. Hebrews interprets Abraham's willingness to sacrifice the child of the promise as an indication of faith in God's ability to bring life even out of death.

The God of the Bible is a God of salvation and liberation, a God who makes covenant with human beings. To believe in such a God means above all to believe in the divine promises and to entrust oneself and one's people to God's continuing care. Biblical faith spills easily over into hope. The God who has done good things in the past will surely do even better things in the future. Such trust leads one to commit oneself to God and to the carrying out of God's will. A covenant always involves a contract between two parties, in this case between God and the people whom God has called.

As much as it emphasizes trust and commitment, biblical faith also includes what might be called an intellectual conviction, the conviction that God exists and is close to, and involved in, human life and especially in the life of Israel. Morning and evening pious Jews affirm their fundamental faith in God in the prayer *Shema Israel:* "Hear, O Israel. The Lord our God is one, he is God and there is no other." Although the biblical understanding of God is multifaceted and is often expressed in symbolic, imaginative, and even anthropomorphic language, over the centuries it was deepened and renewed especially by the prophets and psalmists. God is powerful and transcendent and demanding and at the same time merciful and loving and full of compassion.

According to the gospel of Mark, the initial preaching of Jesus can be summed up as follows: "The time is fulfilled; the kingdom of God has come near; repent, and believe in the good news" (Mk 1:15). Jesus asks two things of his hearers: repentance or conversion, and faith. *Metanoia,* conversion, suggests a change of mind and heart. Jesus invites people to turn, as it were, from what they are doing, to turn from themselves to God and to the offer that God is making through Jesus of forgiveness and of fulfillment. The kingdom of God means many things in the Bible. Although it will only be realized in its fullness in the future, it entails a real gift here and now. People are invited to open themselves to it and to commit themselves to the renewed way of life for which it calls. Faith is crucial in this process. We need to believe that God is in fact present with Jesus and is effecting something through him. Conversion implies a willingness to follow Jesus, to entrust ourselves to him.

In the synoptic gospels faith has a great deal to do with trust. The disciples who are afraid of a storm at sea or who worry about food and drink are chided as persons of little faith. Jesus' healing and forgiving ministry presupposes a trust that God through Jesus is willing to help those who, aware of their need, seek God's help.

Explicit Christian faith, we saw in the last chapter, really only begins with the experience of the resurrection of Jesus. His death and resurrection, the paschal mystery, form the heart of the original apostolic preaching. On Pentecost Peter, having briefly evoked both the public life of Jesus and his death, announces: "This Jesus God raised up" and has made him "both Lord and Messiah" (Acts 2:32, 36). Peter's presentation of the gospel to Cornelius, the pagan centurion, follows the same structure while going into more detail about Jesus' ministry. The climax is once again the death and resurrection. Peter explains that God has made him a witness of these events and has commanded him "to preach to the people and to testify that [Jesus] is the one ordained by God as judge of the living and the dead. All the prophets testify about him that everyone who believes in him receives forgiveness of sins through his name" (Acts 10:42–43).

The faith of the first Christians is rooted in traditional biblical faith in the God of Abraham and Sarah, of Moses and the prophets, the God of creation and of the covenant. What was new was the affirmation that this same God was present in a special way with Jesus and that through God's graciousness Jesus had triumphed over death and had become for all human beings a means of forgiveness and salvation. Christian faith included faith in Jesus as the Messiah, as the risen Lord, as the Son of God, as a unique source of revelation and of new life.

DIMENSIONS OF FAITH IN THE NEW TESTAMENT

St. Paul developed the theme of faith and emphasized its importance for Christian life more than any other of the writers of the New Testament. He seems to have been partly provoked to do so by conflict with so-called Judaizers. These were Christians of Jewish background who insisted that converts from paganism should be obliged to embrace the Mosaic law, including, for males, circumcision. Paul adamantly rejected such views. His letter to the Galatians reveals the emotional intensity of his commitment to the gospel and to his converts, and his bitter disappointment that some of them should be abandoning the freedom to which they were called and submitting themselves to what he describes as the slavery of the law. "You foolish Galatians!" he writes. "Who has bewitched you.... Did you receive the Spirit by doing the works of the law or by believing what you heard?" (Gal 3:1-2). For Paul, the choice is clear-cut: either salvation is through the law or it is through Christ. "Listen! I, Paul, am telling you that if you let yourselves be circumcised, Christ will be of no benefit to you.... You who want to be justified by the law have cut yourselves off from Christ, you have fallen away from grace.... For in Christ Jesus neither circumcision nor uncircumcision counts for anything: the only thing that counts is faith working through love" (Gal 5:2-6).

What Paul expresses so spontaneously and with such passion in Galatians he comes back to in a more reflective and thought-out way in Romans. The basic conviction is spelled out in the first chapter. The gospel "is the power of God for salvation to everyone who has faith, to the Jew first and also to the Greek. For in it the righteousness of God is revealed through faith for faith; as it is written, 'The one who is righteous will live by faith'" (Rom 1:16-17). In subsequent chapters Paul comes back repeatedly to the same basic theme. Before God everyone is a sinner, everyone stands in need of God's grace. We are justified or made righteous not by our efforts, not by works of the law, but by God's grace and by faith in Christ Jesus. If salvation and justification begin with God, the God of creation and of the covenant, the focus of Paul's faith is very much the person of Christ. "It is Christ Jesus who died, yes, who was raised, who is at the right hand of God, who indeed intercedes for us" (Rom 8:34). To the question "Who will separate us from the love of Christ?" (v. 35), Paul answers, "Neither death, nor life... nor things present, nor things to come... nor height, nor depth, nor anything else in all creation, will be able to separate us from the love of God in Christ Jesus our Lord" (Rom 8:38-39).

Faith, for Paul, as for the biblical tradition before him, is the fundamental attitude of a religious person vis-à-vis the God of salvation. Because God's saving act is now focused on the person and destiny of Jesus, so also is the response of faith. It is a response that involves trust and commitment and a willingness to let go of the desire to be the source of our own salvation. It also entails an element of belief, belief in particular that God through the death and resurrection of Jesus has indeed offered humanity justification and wholeness and the gift of the Spirit.

That the content of faith for Paul is not indifferent comes out dramatically in his reaction to what was happening among the Galatians. In the abandonment of Paul's preaching they "are turning to a different gospel—not that there is another gospel, but there are some who are confusing you and want to pervert the gospel of Christ" (Gal 1:6–7). Paul's advice here is categorical: "Even if we or an angel from heaven should proclaim to you a gospel contrary to what we proclaimed to you, let that one be accursed!" (Gal 1:6–8). The Greek word used here is anathema, a word that will come back on many occasions in the history of Christianity.

In chapter 15 of 1 Corinthians, Paul has to deal with doubts that have arisen in the local community about the resurrection of the dead. He begins by appealing to the tradition of the church. He cites a brief formulation of faith, which he says he himself received and handed on to them. It affirms "that Christ died for our sins in accordance with the scriptures, and that he was buried, and that he was raised on the third day in accordance with the scriptures, and that he appeared to Cephas, then to the twelve" (1 Cor 15:3–5). Paul goes on to argue that if, as people say, there is no resurrection of the dead, then Christ has not been raised, and if he has not been raised, then forgiveness has not been granted and faith in him is in vain.

What these texts in Galatians and 1 Corinthians bring out is the fundamental importance that Paul attributes to the content of faith. The gospel is good news because of what it tells us about God and about what God has done for us and for the world in Christ. Part of our acceptance of God's gift is an acceptance of the truth revealed through Christ.

It is partly the seriousness with which Paul takes the content of faith that stimulates him to be as creative and imaginative as he is in the way he presents it. If Christianity includes a vision of God and the world and human life, if it has something to feed the mind as well as the heart, if it calls people to a set of attitudes and actions on the basis of a specific belief, then it is important that those who preach the gospel are able to formulate it in ways that will enable it to reach people where they are, ways that will help them to discern and understand the message and to recognize its implications for their lives. Faith, from the perspective of both the believer and the preacher, calls out for theological development.

Theology in a broad sense has been described in the Catholic tradition as faith seeking understanding. It is not philosophy for its own sake; it is certainly not a form of rationalism. It begins with faith, but it is not satisfied with simple formulations or with a somewhat vague religious attitude. It tries to understand the message of the gospel, to relate it to contemporary experience and culture, to discern the hidden connections among its different parts, to unpack its deeper meaning.

Paul was an enormously creative theologian. He seems, for example, to have been the first Christian to have recognized in the ritual of baptism a symbolic burial with Christ, "so that, just as Christ was raised from the dead... so we too might walk in newness of life" (Rom 6:4). He was also the first to use the image of the body of Christ to suggest the interdependence and the profound bond among the members of the church. What he says in Galatians and Romans about the priority of grace and about justification by faith has stimulated believers and thinkers from the time of Augustine to the present. In 1 Corinthians 15, Paul does not restrict himself to a simple repetition of the traditional faith in regard to the resurrection. He develops an argument that is clearly meant to respond to the type of difficulties that such a belief presented for Christians from a Greek background. He cannot prove the resurrection, but he can suggest an analogy. He appeals to a phenomenon of nature. A seed planted in the ground needs to die before it can bear fruit, and the fruit that it bears has little resemblance to the original seed. "So it is with the resurrection of the dead. What is sown is perishable, what is raised is imperishable. It is sown in dishonor, it is raised in glory. It is sown in weakness, it is raised in power. It is sown a physical body, it is raised a spiritual body" (1 Cor 15:42–44). The purpose of a reflection like this is to eliminate false understandings of the doctrine and to facilitate its acceptance by appealing to what medieval theologians will call an argument of suitability. It does not prove anything, but it does help a person to think about, and to recognize a certain reasonableness in, what he or she is being asked to believe.

Paul is not the only creative theologian in the New Testament. There are several others, especially John and the author of Hebrews. Each of these offers a distinctive perspective on the mystery of Christ and on the meaning of his life and destiny for us. The gospel of John emphasizes love and eternal life. Jesus is the Word of God incarnate who in his love reveals the great love of God for the world. The first letter of John, on the basis of the gospel, affirms that God is love and that those who abide in love abide in God. We come to God through Christ; he is the bread of life, the water that springs up to eternal life. Eternal life begins now for those who believe in Jesus and in the Father who sent him.

Like Paul, the author of Hebrews focuses on the death and resurrection of Jesus but interprets it in a different way. He emphasizes the language of priesthood and Temple and sacrifice. Jesus is a great high priest who, unlike the high priests of the Temple of Jerusalem, who entered the holy of holies every year on the day of atonement to offer expiation for sins, "entered once for all into the Holy Place, not with the blood of goats and calves, but with his own blood, thus obtaining eternal redemption" (Heb 9:12). His sacrifice was above all the obedience and love that marked his life and which came to their climax in his death on the cross. "By a single offering he has perfected for all time those who are sanctified" (Heb 10:14). Having entered the heavenly temple, Christ remains there forever interceding on our behalf. Such a vision is meant to offer comfort and assurance to believers facing persecution and temptation. "Since we have a great priest over the house of God, let us approach with a true heart in full assurance of faith.... Let us hold fast to the confession of our hope without wavering.... And let us consider how to provoke one another to love and good deeds" (Heb 10:21–24).

For Catholics, as for most Christians, the Bible remains the most important single source and norm for their faith and life. As human as it obviously is, Christians think of it as the word of God because its authors were inspired by God's Spirit to write what they did. To know the Christian scriptures is to know how different are the points of view and the theologies of those who wrote them. They lived in different communities faced with a variety of challenges and difficulties and they tried to respond to them in the way in which they presented the gospel message. If there is a single content to Christian faith, and if that content is focused on Christ and on the salvation that comes from God through him, there are at the same time many ways of under-standing it, many aspects of life to which it needs to be related, different religious and philosophical and other categories that can be used to illuminate it. This explains the difference within unity that marks the distinctive theologies of Paul and John and of the letter to the Hebrews. Unity of faith is open to and requires a plurality of formulations. Only thus can the one gospel reach people where they are.

GUARDING THE FAITH ONCE GIVEN

The authentic letters of Paul reflect what is obviously a cre-ative moment in the development of early Christianity. Although he is adamant about the importance of the content of faith, Paul tends to emphasize in his preaching its subjective meaning. Faith for him describes our global response to God turned to us in Christ. It includes belief but, even more, trust and self- giving obe-dience and love. By the end of the first century the emphasis in the New Testament shifted, perhaps nowhere more obviously than in certain writings attributed to Paul, the letters to Timothy and to Titus, which seem to have been written some twenty years after his death. Here the concern is with the content of faith and with the need to protect it from distortions and false understandings. Timo-thy, as a kind of ideal disciple and successor of Paul, is encouraged to "hold to the standard of sound teaching that you have heard from me" and to "entrust [it] to faithful people who will be able to teach others as well" (2 Tm 1:14, 2:2). There are those in the com-munity "who have swerved from the truth.... They are upsetting the faith of some" (2 Tm 2:18). Those who do such things are "wicked people and impostors [who] will go from bad to worse, deceiving others and being deceived" (2 Tm 3:13). Timothy is warned to continue steadfast in what he has learned from his childhood. He is above all to read the scriptures and to proclaim them to others.

Paul's final words to Timothy give expression to a broader concern that runs through many of the New Testament writings, a concern that the gospel not be distorted or betrayed or undermined in the process of preaching and teaching it to successive generations. To underline the seriousness of what he is saying, Paul evokes both the final judgment and his own approaching death. With conscious solemnity he enjoins his younger colleague:

> Proclaim the message; be persistent whether the time is favorable or unfavorable; convince, rebuke, and encourage, with the utmost patience in teaching. For the time is coming when people will not put up with sound doctrine, but having itching ears, they will accumulate for themselves teachers to suit their own desires, and will turn away from listening to the truth and wander away to myths. (2 Tm 4:2–4)

According to the universal teaching of the New Testament, faith is at the heart of Christian life. As a fundamental religious attitude it evokes the kind of global response to the revealing and saving activity of God in Jesus Christ that distinguishes the true disciple. It entails an assent of the mind, an act of belief, and even more a commitment of the whole person to Christ and to God. It implies a way of life suggested by words like service and love. To be a believer is to be a disciple, and to be a disciple involves an ethical stance and a religious attitude as well as a deep-rooted conviction about the truth of the gospel.

FOSTERING THE LIFE OF FAITH

The Catholic tradition has always put a considerable emphasis on what might be called the life of faith. Catechetics and the liturgy, forms of prayers and of private devotion, churches and their decorations, these and other things have been developed so that in different ways they might foster and encourage and deepen the life of faith of individual believers. Religious orders, whether contemplative or active, have always had as a primary purpose to contribute to the spiritual life of their members and the community. The vows of poverty, chastity, and obedience, as well as the details of the various religious rules of life, are meant to serve individual and community growth in prayer and virtue. Saints have always played a large part in Catholic history. In recognizing their holiness and in offering them to the veneration and the imitation of believers, church authorities have underlined in every age the necessity of the pursuit of Christian perfection.

Catholics think of the life of faith as beginning in a special way at baptism and then growing over the years in response to God's gifts, to ethical and religious effort and to continuing involvement in the sacramental life of the church. In recent years there has been a renewed interest in Christian mysticism and in the writings and lives of those who have been recognized as having lived the common Christian life, especially in terms of prayer and religious experience, with a particular intensity. Whether finally canonized or not, such people are clearly a major element in the Catholic tradition. Serious study of their lives and writings is bringing home in a new way how richly over the centuries the Catholic Church in its own distinctive ways has nourished the life of faith.

As important as this life is, the rest of the present chapter will focus on something that in comparison with some other traditions is, I believe, even more characteristic of Catholicism; namely, its concern for the content of faith, both with maintaining it and with bringing it creatively into contact with changing cultures and situations.

DEVELOPING THE CREEDS

The Bible is more like a library containing a wide range of works than a single book. The New Testament alone is made up of twenty-seven documents written over a period of fifty or more years and reflecting a number of different communities, situations, and theological perspectives. For much of church history very few Catholics would have ever had access to the biblical texts except within the liturgy. What was needed from the beginning was some kind of brief summary of biblical faith, something that believers could memorize and repeat and teach to their children. This seems to have been at least part of the motivation that led to the development of the creeds. The English word *creed* comes from the Latin *credo,* "I believe." Creeds are brief statements of Christian faith. The forerunners of the Apostles' Creed go back at least to the mid-second century. Although many communities developed their own forms of the creed, these all tended rather rapidly to take on more or less the same pattern.

As mentioned in chapter 2, the creeds are trinitarian in structure. The general consensus is that they developed in the context of baptism and its preparation. Adult converts who were to be baptized in the name of the Father, Son, and Spirit were asked to profess their faith in the same triune God. And so the creeds took the form that we know today. They proclaim faith in God the Father, the creator, in his Son Jesus Christ, the redeemer, and in the Holy Spirit, active in the church in bringing about the forgiveness of sins and the resurrection of the body and life everlasting.

Short formulas of faith can be found in a number of writings within the New Testament, especially in Paul. More often than not these focus on the person of Christ and on his death and resurrection. The one that appears in 1 Corinthians 15:4–6 has already been quoted. Romans 1:2–4 in all probability contains at least a paraphrase of another such early creedal formulation. Paul presents himself as "an apostle set apart for the gospel of God, which he promised beforehand through his prophets in the holy scriptures, the gospel concerning his Son, who was descended from David according to the flesh and was declared to be Son of God with power according to the Spirit of holiness by resurrection from the dead, Jesus Christ our Lord" (Rom 1:1–4). The pastoral letters, as one might expect, also contain such short, apparently traditional statements of faith. The letter of 1 Timothy 2:5–6 affirms:

> There is one God;
> there is also one mediator between God and humankind,
> Christ Jesus, himself human,
> who gave himself a ransom for all.

The way in which the traditional creeds have synthesized and focused the breadth of the New Testament message has had a dramatic influence on subsequent Christian and especially Catholic understandings of the faith. Profoundly trinitarian, the creed affirms the reality of, and the distinctions among, Father, Son, and Spirit. At the same time it has a built-in sensitivity to what is often referred to as the history of salvation. Everything begins with God's creative activity. The coming of Jesus Christ marks a new and definitive stage in God's relationship to humanity. The Spirit continues Christ's work and enables it to bear its intended fruit, above all in the community of faith. This fruit will include eventually the resurrection of the body and the final triumph of God's kingdom. As brief as it is, the creed encompasses everything, it embraces God, the world, and human life, it reaches from creation to the end of time.

THE STRUGGLE WITH HERESY

In the section in 1 Corinthians in which he deals with abuses that have arisen around the community celebration of the eucharist, Paul comments: "I hear that there are divisions among you; and to some extent I believe it. Indeed, there have to be factions among you, for only so will it become clear who among you are genuine" (1 Cor 11:18–19). The original Greek words that are translated here as "divisions" and "factions" are *schismata* and *haireseis* respectively. In interpreting this passage later theologians will give these terms a more technical meaning than they had for Paul. "Heresy" will refer not to just any kind of faction or division but to a deviation from Christian orthodoxy. The original Greek for heresy suggests an element of choice, a choosing to separate oneself from others or the choice of one sect as opposed to another. Christians will charge "heretics" with choosing part of the gospel message rather than accepting it as a whole, or with choosing some philosophy or other perspective rather than the revelation handed down in the tradition of the church. Paul's remark about the necessity of "heresies" became a principle by which people interpreted the history of doctrine.

Heresy forced the church to make decisions and in doing so to clarify the content of its faith.

The great doctrinal debates of the early church focused above all on the person of Christ and on the mystery of the Trinity. The affirmation of the prologue of the gospel of John that in Jesus the eternal logos or Word of God became flesh was a crucial element in the way in which Christian teachers and preachers presented the person of Christ within the Hellenistic world. Converts from paganism knew relatively little about the Jewish tradition and about the significance, for example, of the Messiah. Those among them, however, who had even a passing acquaintance with Greek philosophy were aware of the concept of the logos. In the philosophical tradition the term meant both word and reason. Some thought of it as an instrument of God's creative activity; others saw it as an immanent principle giving meaning and unity to the cosmos. The fact that humans too share in the logos gives them a capacity to know God and to discern the unifying pattern at the heart of the world.

Second-century Christian apologists, in explaining and defending their faith to adherents of Hellenistic philosophy and culture, presented Christ primarily as the Word incarnate. They claimed that the logos about which philosophy already spoke had taken on human form in Jesus. That same Word, they affirmed, was present in the Greek tradition and had inspired what was best in it. To become Christians, therefore, Greeks did not have to turn their back on their own culture, but were able to bring it to fulfillment. Ideas like these merited for Justin and other apologists the title of the first Christian theologians after the New Testament writers themselves. The openness and creativity of their efforts to articulate the gospel in terms of the culture of their day have remained a model to which Catholicism continues to appeal. For present purposes what is important is not only the overall approach of the apologists but also the way in which they made the logos, the Word, the key to christology.

The affirmation that in Christ the Word was made flesh inevitably raised questions, questions that would gradually become more pressing until they threatened to divide the church in irreversible ways. A first set of questions had to do with the

Word in itself and in its relation to God. What precisely is meant in this context by the *Word?* What is being affirmed when it is said that the Word is God? Is it simply a way of talking about the one God, a way, for example, of referring to God's self-revelation to humanity, or does it point to a distinction within God between God and God's Word? If there is a real distinction between the two, are they equal, or is one subordinate to the other, or are they perhaps two Gods? Or should one go even further and affirm that although the Word transcends all other creatures, it is itself, finally, not divine but a part of creation?

People took these questions seriously, and in the course of the second and third centuries various answers were given and gradually certain common convictions developed. The issue came to a crisis at the beginning of the fourth century. A presbyter named Arius in Alexandria argued that the Word who had become flesh in Jesus and who had undergone suffering and death could not possibly be divine. God, for Arius, so transcends the world and every kind of limitation, especially ignorance and death, that he could never have taken on human form. The Word is thus not God but rather a creature, the highest of all possible creatures, but still a creature. He stands on this side of the great divide between God and what is not God. Nor is the Word eternal. "There was a time when he was not."

When Arius's bishop, Alexander, condemned his thinking and censored him for it, Arius appealed to other bishops from neighboring dioceses who supported him. In spite of attempts to resolve the conflict, it continued to grow until Emperor Constantine, who had recently granted legal status to the church, intervened and demanded that the bishops act and end the controversy. The last thing he wanted was for the church to be a source of division within the empire.

ECUMENICAL COUNCILS

Constantine's solution was to call together all the bishops, at least of the eastern part of the church, to a great council that was finally held in 325 in Nicaea in Asia Minor. The council came to be regarded as the first of the ecumenical councils.

The early church had no developed interchurch organizational structure. There was no centralized bureaucracy. Local churches tended to be largely independent under the leadership of their bishop. Some churches, especially those which claimed apostolic origin, were regarded as having special status. By the fourth century, Rome, Alexandria, and Antioch were all recognized as exercising a certain primacy over other churches in their respective areas. All three were important cities in the empire, and all were connected in different ways with the apostle Peter. The church of Rome claimed first place for itself because both Peter and Paul had preached and been martyred there. The church of Constantinople made a claim of its own in the course of the fourth and fifth centuries based on the city's status as the new Rome, the new capital of the empire.

By the latter half of the second century synods and councils of bishops were taking place in Asia Minor. Such a development seems natural and indeed inevitable. Problems and conflicts arose that had ramifications beyond a single church. Bishops gathered to consult one another and to come to common decisions about what should be done. The practice became relatively common in the course of the third century. We hear, for example, of meetings of bishops being held on a regular basis in North Africa during the period when Cyprian was bishop of Carthage (249–59).

The Greek root of the word *ecumenical* means "the inhabited world." To call the gathering of bishops that took place at Nicaea an ecumenical council is to distinguish it from the innumerable local councils that had preceded it. The conflict that Arius unleashed had gone beyond a single church or even a single region and was beginning to disturb the church as a whole. The issue that he and his supporters brought to the fore was crucial for all believers. And so Constantine determined to have a truly universal council. In fact, although recognized as ecumenical and although its decisions had a determining influence on the whole of subsequent church history, it was largely a council of Eastern bishops. Only a few bishops from the Latin West decided to attend and they were accompanied by two presbyters representing Pope Sylvester.

The council condemned Arius and added some clarifying phrases to a traditional baptismal creed. The second article now read:

> And in one Lord Jesus Christ, the Son of God, the only begotten, begotten from the Father, that is, from the substance of the Father, God from God, light from light, true God from true God, begotten not made, consubstantial with the Father, through whom all things came to be, both those in heaven and those on earth; for us humans and for our salvation he came down and became incarnate, becoming human, suffered and rose up on the third day, went up into the heavens, and is coming to judge the living and the dead.

Although the desire is clearly to affirm the divinity of the Word, who became incarnate in Jesus, the term *Word* is avoided and is replaced by the even more traditional language of *Son*. The Son is begotten from the very substance of the Father, begotten and not made and therefore truly God. The most controversial phrase in the formulation then and since is the one translated here as "consubstantial with the Father." The key Greek term is *homoousios*, a word that Constantine himself apparently insisted should be included. It was a technical word, a non-biblical one, and one that was open to misunderstanding. It became an occasion for continuing debate and division.

The council of Nicaea is an important moment in the development of Catholic Christianity. It began a tradition of ecumenical councils whose doctrinal definitions are regarded as secondary only to the scriptures as a norm of Christian faith. Nicaea was the first of several largely Greek-speaking councils to which Catholics and Orthodox as well as many Anglicans and some Protestants look back as defining moments in the developing formulation of their faith. The Catholic Church sees the tradition of the early councils, begun at Nicaea, as continuing in its own history. The most important moments in this ongoing conciliar tradition have been the councils of Trent (1545–63), Vatican I (1869–70), and Vatican II (1962–65). Although some theologians have raised questions about the full ecumenicity of councils held after the division of East and West and after the further divisions that followed upon the Protestant Reformation, the three councils just mentioned have had a decisive impact on Catholic identity in terms of both faith and practice. Even today, Catholics from very different backgrounds believe that another general council will be necessary to deal with some of the internal church matters and ecumenical issues that will have to be faced in the not too distant future.

AN EMPHASIS ON ORTHODOXY

The word *orthodoxy* has come to mean "right faith, right belief." An orthodox person is one who holds the true faith of the church, in contrast to the heretic who in some way or other has rejected or turned away from it. The Arian crisis and the calling of the council of Nicaea seem to have resulted in a greater emphasis being put on orthodoxy than ever before. If faith is central to the church, agreement about faith is a crucial factor in maintaining and fostering church unity.

As clear-cut as the condemnation of Arius was at Nicaea, the result of the council was not the one for which Constantine had been hoping. Bishops disagreed about its positive teaching and especially about the implications of the word *homoousios*. The divisions continued for some twenty to thirty years, and when they were finally overcome a new conflict broke out around the person of the Holy Spirit. Questions were raised about the Spirit that were analogous to those which had been debated earlier about the Word. Once again the questioning and the conflict stimulated a development in theology that bore its fruit in a council held in Constantinople in 381, a council that came to be regarded as the second ecumenical council. It reaffirmed the teaching of Nicaea and added to its formulation of the creed a more extensive section on the Holy Spirit. What we call the Nicene Creed is the product of both of these great councils, its section on Christ having been formulated at Nicaea and that on the Holy Spirit at Constantinople.

The work of these two councils, not only in clarifying Christian faith in the Trinity but in giving formulation to it within the context of the traditional creed, helped to give the creed a new meaning. Earlier forms of the creed were shorter and simpler and reflected the baptismal context in which they had grown up. The Nicene Creed, on the other hand, was the result of theological controversy and debate and of the decisions of bishops gathered in council. One might call it an episcopal creed, a creed whose purpose is to act as a measure or criterion for orthodoxy. It provided bishops with a handy summary of Catholic faith precisely in regard to those areas in which there had been the greatest conflict.

The fourth-century controversy about the Trinity was paralleled by a series of debates that came to a head in the fifth century and that focused on the person of Christ. If the Word who became flesh in Jesus is truly divine, one of the three persons within the one God, how are we to conceive the relationship in Jesus between the divine and the human? Is the unity between the two so intense that we can hardly imagine how Jesus might have suffered or not known something or experienced anguish in the face of death? In other words, did the presence of the divine in Jesus tend to undermine the fullness of his humanity? Or should we think of the unity between God and human in Jesus more in terms of a moral unity? In this case Jesus would be a human being like us in everything except in his extraordinary holiness, his unique obedience to and love of God. Should Mary be called the mother of God or simply the mother of Christ?

After the council of Ephesus in 431 defended the practice of calling Mary the *theotokos,* the mother of God, a fourth council was called in 451 at Chalcedon in order to address the larger issue of Jesus' identity and of the relation of the divine and human in him. The council did not add anything to the creed but rather produced a brief statement that became widely regarded as the orthodox formulation of faith in Christ. It affirms the fundamental unity of Christ, "truly God and truly man," consubstantial to the Father in regard to divinity and consubstantial to us in regard to humanity. He is

> one and the same Christ, Son, Lord, only-begotten, acknowledged in two natures which undergo no confusion, no change, no division, no separation; at no point was the difference between the two natures taken away through the union, but rather the property of both natures is preserved and comes together into a single person and into a single subsistent being (one *prosopon* and one *hypostasis*).

From this very careful and nuanced and to some degree negatively formulated statement, the subsequent tradition tended to focus on the idea of the two natures, human and divine, united in the one person of the divine Word or Son. This has remained a key component of Catholic orthodoxy to the present day.

It would be difficult to exaggerate the importance for Catholic faith of the work of the early councils. They reinforced and deepened and gave more precise formulation to two of the major components of the baptismal creed: the Trinity and the incarnation. Modern scholarship is helping us to recognize the complexity of the positions and debates that led to the conciliar definitions. The way the questions were put, the categories and language used, the very process by which the conciliar decisions came to be agreed upon, were all historically conditioned. This kind of knowledge helps us to understand better what the councils were able to achieve and what their limits were. The heritage of this formative period in Catholic history is certainly open to further development, but it cannot be simply rejected or disregarded. Catholicism, as it has traditionally understood itself, cannot go behind the work of those councils that have come to be regarded as ecumenical. Their doctrinal decisions remain a vital part of Catholic tradition, a criterion, after and dependent on the scriptures, of orthodox Catholic faith.

THE IMPORTANCE OF THEOLOGY

Taken in the broadest sense, theology in the Christian tradition entails thinking about and trying to understand our faith and the faith of the church. Faith and theology belong together. To believe in God includes a belief in what has been revealed in Christ about God, the world, and the meaning of human life. Divine revelation cries out to be thought about and to be related to all that we know and imagine from other sources, from science and philosophy and from the history of human culture. Theology is particularly important for the life of the church. It helps church leaders and ministers of every kind to deepen their insight into the faith and to overcome false understandings of it;

it serves the task of preaching and of helping successive generations of believers to bring faith into relation with new and changing situations. Theology, like everything human in the church,
can fail in different ways: it can be less than intelligent, it can be
cowardly, it can be presumptuous. Theologians can fail in their
responsibilities by refusing to allow themselves to be challenged
by new cultures and questions; they can fail, too, by an inadequate appreciation for the tradition, by disregarding, for example, the authentic message of the scriptures or by not doing
justice to the defined doctrines of the church.

Reference has already been made to the remarkable theological activity of New Testament writers like John and Paul and
the author of Hebrews. What they did in their context was continued in an analogous way and in dependence on them by second-century apologists and by the great theologians of the
patristic period.

Over the centuries Catholic theology has taken a variety of
forms and been developed in a number of quite different contexts. In and through all the variety, one can recognize the high
priority that Catholicism has given to theology. Its service to the
faith and to the life of the church has been and remains crucial.

In the early church there were no Catholic universities or
seminaries. Most of the great theologians of the time were bishops who developed their theology in close connection with the
concrete pastoral life of the communities for which they had
responsibility. Their theology can be found in their sermons,
especially those addressed to catechumens or recent converts or
those that marked the great feasts of the liturgical year. They
wrote against heresies or in defense of the teachings of the councils. A bishop like Augustine went further than most in trying to
relate the Catholic faith to what was best in the science and philosophy and history of his day. The distinctive accents of his theology reflect both his own life and personality and the specific
church issues with which as a bishop he had to deal.

Some of the most important theology of the early medieval
period was developed in monasteries. Its function was above all to
serve monks and nuns in their reading of scripture and in their
efforts to live a life of intense prayer and spirituality. Theology

took on a new form and a different tone with the rise of the universities in the twelfth and thirteenth centuries. University theology came to be known as Scholasticism. It was no longer as clearly related to the pastoral life of the church as theology had been in the patristic period, nor was it meant directly to serve the liturgical and prayer life of monks; it was more scholarly, more objective, more rational. Some of the greatest Scholastic theologians tried to develop a synthesis between Christian faith and all the philosophical and other knowledge that was available in the period. The involvement of the church and of theology in the development of the medieval university reveals a great deal about a perennial Catholic conviction in regard to reason and faith. Faith may go beyond reason, but it does not deny its capacities and value; neither does it contradict the truth that reason is able to discover. Much of medieval Catholic theology rejoiced in reason and truth and in the positive relationship that it believed could be established between human knowledge and the truth of faith. All truth comes from God and reflects in some way God's very being. Faith does not undermine human reason but rather affirms it and encourages it to seek the truth.

Thomas Aquinas, a thirteenth-century Dominican theologian and professor at the University of Paris, came to epitomize for centuries the Catholic understanding of the relationship between faith and reason. He lived at a moment of great intellectual and social upheaval. A new world of thought was opening up in the Europe of his day. Traditionally, Catholic theology had recourse to various forms of Platonic philosophy in its efforts to reflect on the scriptures and the creed. Increased contact in the thirteenth century between Arab and Christian thinkers resulted among other things in a rediscovery in the Latin world of the philosophy of Aristotle. Many people rejected the new philosophy as too materialistic or too rationalistic to be helpful in theology. Thomas, however, saw in Aristotle a thinker who in many ways had understood reality better than anyone else, and so he sought ways of bringing what was best in Aristotle's philosophy into a positive and fruitful dialogue with Christian faith. The result was a new and creative systematic presentation of the Catholic world view. Although many were initially scandalized at

Thomas's boldness, subsequent generations came to recognize in his theology one of the great achievements in the history of Christian thought.

Theology did not stop with Aquinas or with the development of medieval Scholasticism. The twentieth century has witnessed a dramatic renewal in Catholic thought in a variety of contexts and forms. Today theology is done in universities and seminaries, by people involved in the Third World with the poor and the oppressed, in centers of spirituality, and in pastoral settings in what until recently were mission countries. Contemporary theologians reflect on the relation between biblical faith and an evolutionary view of the world, between Christian life and the theories of modern psychology, between the Christian teaching about the kingdom of God and modern political and sociological perspectives, between traditional formulations of the faith and the experiences and concerns of Christian women.

Theologians are by no means the only teachers in the church. Catholicism has always attributed a special and authoritative role to what is called the magisterium, the teaching office that is part of the larger pastoral responsibilities of the bishops and the pope. Much of what could and should be said on this topic will have to wait for chapter 5, which will focus more directly on the question of the ordained ministry and on the hierarchical structure of the church. For now let it simply be said that theology in the Catholic tradition is never merely a private thing. The faith about which theologians primarily think is the faith of the church. Their efforts at understanding it and relating it to other aspects of human knowledge and culture are meant to help all members of the church, both lay and ordained, to deepen their faith life and to fulfill their mission and ministry. If theologians are to make the contribution of which they are capable, they need to be in dialogue with the magisterium and respectful of its authority and responsibility. On the other hand, as the example of the close collaboration of theologians and bishops at Vatican II has shown, the magisterium needs the help and stimulation of theologians if it is to fulfill its task, not only to preserve the faith once given but to find ways to make it, in a changed historical situation, the ever creative source of new and renewed Christian life.

INDEFECTIBILITY AND INFALLIBILITY

Central to Catholic faith is the conviction that the church is more than simply the coming together of believers in response to the preaching of the gospel; it is a part of God's plan of salvation, an instrument chosen and created by God to keep alive in the world in a visible and tangible form the revelation and grace that are given in Christ. Here is the basis for the church's conviction about the continuing presence of the Holy Spirit in the church. In spite of sin and failure and all the inevitable inadequacies that haunt everything human, the church trusts that it will not succumb to the powers of darkness. Jesus at a solemn and critical moment in his public ministry declared to Simon Peter: "You are Peter, and on this rock I will build my church, and the gates of Hades will not prevail against it" (Mt 16:18).

Catholic confidence in this *indefectibility* of the church rests not on church leaders or church structures but on the promise of Christ and on the presence of God's Spirit within the community of faith. Because the truth of the gospel is so central to the Catholic understanding of Christianity, over the centuries Catholic thinkers have come to apply this promise and this help in a special way to the area of church teaching. In spite of all intellectual and moral limitations, the church as church cannot fall away from the substance or the essence of the gospel. Since the medieval period, theologians have spoken of the infallibility of the church.

The word *infallibility* suggests an incapacity to be wrong in judging something to be true or not, a protection against falling into error. That church members, including theologians and saints as well as bishops and popes, have erred in many ways in the course of history led theologians to try to determine more precisely what was being affirmed by the language of infallibility. Vatican I (1869–70) for the first time defined the infallible nature of the teaching authority of the pope. That the great councils of the church had been infallible in their doctrinal affirmations had long been held. Here that same infallibility, which the council says Christ intended as a gift for the whole church, was said to be exercised in a special way by the pope when, in an official act as the chief pastor and teacher of the church, he solemnly defines a truth of faith or morals as belonging to the content of God's revelation. The conditions on which the council insisted for such an infallible definition make clear that it is a rare occurrence in the life of the church. Infallibility, moreover, is no guarantee that the formulation given is the best possible one or that its definition at a particular moment is a pastorally wise action. It guarantees, rather, that through the assistance of the Spirit such a definition is not false, that it does not go against the truth of the gospel. The way, over time, that a particular definition is received into the life of the church tells a great deal about its precise meaning and its final authority. Debates, for example, about what exactly Vatican I defined in this area have continued into the present. Many theologians see the exercise of papal infallibility as extremely rare. The one clear example of it since 1870 is the definition by Pius XII in 1950 of the dogma of the assumption of Mary.

Vatican II reaffirmed and developed the teaching of Vatican I on papal infallibility and related it to the role of bishops. "Although the bishops, taken individually, do not enjoy the privilege of infallibility, they do, however, proclaim infallibly the doctrine of Christ" when, even though dispersed around the world, they remain in contact with other bishops and the pope and with them affirm that a particular teaching of faith and morals "is to be held definitively and absolutely." (*Dogmatic Constitution on the Church,* no. 25) They exercise this authority in a particularly solemn way when they are gathered together in an ecumenical council. But even here, we have to be attentive to the express intention that the bishops have. At Vatican II, for example, no claim was made that any new doctrine was being infallibly defined and taught.

The notion of infallibility is a difficult and complex one. In the strict sense of the word only God is infallible. If there is any guarantee of infallibility outside of God, it is because of a gift from God that is meant to serve and protect and hand on the truth of revelation. It is not something that applies to everything that church leaders say and do. Nor is it to be thought of apart from the slow and laborious struggle to discover the truth that is part of the human condition. The gift of infallibility, moreover, relates not only to teaching but also to believing. Vatican II affirms that "the whole body of the faithful... cannot err in matters of belief" (*Dogmatic Constitution on the Church,* no. 12). It appeals to what has traditionally been called the *sensus fidei,* a religious appreciation of the faith shared in by all the baptized. All are endowed with the gift of the Spirit and are helped to discern the truth of the gospel. It is for this reason that the exercise of episcopal and papal infallibility requires a prior consultation of the laity and for this reason too that the subsequent reception by the community of faith of defined truths helps to determine their precise significance.

In spite of the difficulties inherent in it, the language of infallibility is important because it points to the Catholic conviction that the truth of revelation is a precious gift to humanity, that God did not simply abandon it to human weakness and caprice. The Spirit of truth accompanies the church on its historical pilgrimage and inspires believers, saints, theologians, and official teachers to collaborate in maintaining and developing the truth of the gospel. The presence of the Spirit protects the revelation given us in Christ from being distorted by human blindness and error.

BUILDING UP THE COMMUNITY OF FAITH

In order to become a member of the church, an adult must first profess a personal faith in God and in God's saving and revealing activity in Christ and through the Spirit. Infants, on the other hand, are baptized in the faith of their parents and of the broader community. In their case baptism calls out for a subsequent program of catechetics and practice that will enable them one day to make their own mature act of faith.

If faith is essential for entering the church, it is also at the heart of our ongoing life in the church. Word and sacrament, prayers and service, all the things that constitute the Christian life presuppose a real and deepening attitude of faith. Without faith almost nothing that the church is and does and claims makes sense.

To be a person of faith in our world is not easy. Our culture, at least on the surface, is strikingly secular. The reality of God

and of Christ is anything but self-evident. For most of us faith
tends to come alive when we undergo profound human experiences like falling in love, or suffering, or becoming conscious
of responsibility for another or confronting death. At such
moments we can awaken to a sense of the mystery that surrounds
and permeates our life and that religious people have always
called God. Contact with real Christians or the scriptures or the
liturgy can help us relate that mystery to the person and life of
Jesus. In his teaching and especially through his death and resurrection he reveals something about God and the meaning of our
lives. We are called to live in friendship and love with him and
with one another.

The church exists to help us deepen and live our faith. As
personal as the relationship that each one of us has with God is,
we are not intended to live it out in isolation but in a community
of believers. Almost everything about the church is meant to
serve and build up our faith. It does this not only by involving us
in personal and liturgical prayer but by seeing that the gospel
message continues to be proclaimed and taught in all its
integrity. To serve this purpose councils have been held, theologians have given their lives to the study of the scriptures and of
the Christian tradition, and bishops and popes have exercised
their distinctive teaching authority. Faith, both as a personal religious attitude or virtue and as the content of God's revelation in
Christ, is at the heart of Catholic life.

CHAPTER FOUR

A Sacramental Community

Something that in the past was probably more regularly regarded as distinctive of Catholicism than almost anything else was the emphasis that the Catholic tradition gave to the sacraments and to involvement in the sacramental life of the church. In the period leading up to Vatican II there was a tendency to contrast Catholic and Protestant forms of Christianity by describing the former as sacramental and the latter as more focused on the word, whether the biblical word or the word of preaching. As simplified and one-sided as the contrast was, it did correspond to some degree to the theological emphases and the actual practice of the different churches.

By the late medieval period the classical Catholic understanding in regard to the sacraments was firmly in place. From the twelfth century on, church teaching affirmed that there were seven sacraments and that they had all been instituted either directly or indirectly by Christ. As such they were privileged vehicles of grace. Their effectiveness did not depend on the goodness or the devotion of the minister but was in a very real sense inherent in them. The technical phrase that was widely used at the time to suggest this intrinsic capacity of the sacraments to effect what they signified was *ex opere operato;* the very fact of positing the sacrament caused grace to flow through it. Sacraments depended primarily on God's activity operating in and through them rather than on any human agency.

The sacramental system touched on all aspects of the life of individuals and of the church community. Through baptism a person was freed from original sin, received the gift of grace, and became a member of the church. Confirmation was administered by the bishop and brought a person to a certain maturity in the

Christian life and to a new level of responsibility in regard to the church community. The eucharist was regarded as both a sacrament and a sacrifice, and in the form of the weekly and daily Mass was the center of the religious life of all serious Catholics. On a popular level, there was more of a preoccupation with the miraculous presence of Christ under the form of the host, which by this time was becoming an object of adoration, than with directly sharing in the eucharist by receiving communion. As a sacrifice the Mass could be offered by the priest for special intentions whether for the living or for the dead. Church law required that people receive the sacrament of penance at least once a year and that they take communion during the Easter season. Extreme Unction, as the name suggested, tended more and more to be restricted to those who were near death. Although the ritual still made mention of the possibility of healing, the emphasis was on forgiveness and on the preparation of the soul for its encounter with God. Both marriage and ordination were viewed as social sacraments, the first consecrating the fundamental human social unit, the family, and the second giving a religious and sacramental meaning to the ordained ministry. According to both late medieval theology and church teaching, only a priest or bishop could offer the sacrifice of the Mass or administer the other sacraments, with the exception of baptism, which anyone, even nonbelievers, might administer as long as they wanted to do what the church intended by the ritual, and with the further exception of marriage, which the Western tradition believed the couple administered to one another in exchanging vows.

FROM THE REFORMATION TO THE COUNCIL OF TRENT

Luther and the other reformers reacted against what they considered to be abuses and distortions in the traditional theory and practice of the sacraments. They rejected the notion of *ex opere operato* as something that on a popular level could easily lead to a magical sense of the sacraments' effectiveness. Their reaction here was part of a broader reaction against the medieval emphasis on the objective nature of the sacraments. The reformers stressed that sacraments in some way proclaim the reality of

Christ's saving work and the forgiveness and new life that it implies. It is by faith that believers open themselves to that reality. As signs, sacraments are meant to stimulate that response.

The application to this area of the general reformation principle of *sola scriptura*—scripture alone as a norm for faith—led the reformers eventually to recognize only two sacraments as instituted by Christ, baptism and the eucharist. Initially Luther maintained penance as well, but he gave it up when he became convinced that it was not firmly based in scripture. Although the reformers kept the eucharist and emphasized its importance for the life of the church, they rejected the Catholic doctrine of transubstantiation, the doctrine that affirms that in the eucharist the substance of the bread and wine becomes the reality of Christ. Luther believed in the presence of Christ in the eucharist, but he could not accept the traditional Catholic explanation of it. The reformers also abandoned the notion of the Mass as a sacrifice. They saw it primarily as a sacrament, as a gift of God to us and not in any sense as something that we are able to offer to God. They judged the Catholic understanding here as taking away from the unique sacrifice of Christ and as in some sense contributing to what Luther called "works righteousness," that is, an approach to religion that puts the emphasis more on our moral and religious efforts than on God's grace.

All the reformers stressed the importance of the Bible and the centrality to Christian worship of readings from it. Preaching was to be given a central place in the liturgy and was to be rooted in the biblical message. This emphasis on the word inevitably brought a demand for a vernacular liturgy. Only a proclamation of the whole of the ritual, including the biblical texts, in the language of the faithful would enable it to nurture their faith as it was intended to do.

This rather massive rejection of so much that was central to the Catholic sacramental tradition led the bishops gathered at the council of Trent (1545–63) to make sacramental theology a priority. They knew that there were abuses that had to be corrected, and they made efforts in order to do so, but their main concern was to respond to the attack of Luther and the others on the theology and practice of the sacraments that had developed over the centuries. The council dealt with the sacraments in all three of its periods (1545–47, 1551, 1562–63), producing statements on the nature of sacraments in general and on the seven individual sacraments. The eucharist was handled at two different sessions, first as a sacrament and then as a sacrifice.

Trent basically reaffirmed in a solemn way the sacramental synthesis that had been formally taught in the medieval period. It offered no compromise even in practical areas, such as the use of the vernacular or in offering the chalice to the laity, areas in which some compromise might have been possible. Because Trent set the tone for the renewal of Catholic life for the next four hundred years, its anti-reformation emphases had a profound influence on modern Catholic identity.

Although Tridentine Catholicism was marked by a number of other characteristics as well, it certainly put a considerable emphasis on a distinctively Catholic understanding of the sacraments and on the responsibility of the laity to participate regularly in them. Good Catholics had their children baptized as soon as possible after birth. They saw to it that they were confirmed at the appropriate time and that they made their first communion. Regular attendance at the Sunday Mass was a mark of serious commitment to the church. In the twentieth century an increasing emphasis was put on weekly communion and therefore on a more regular practice of the sacrament of penance. Catholics took for granted that their marriage would receive a church blessing and that it would be recognized as a sacrament. Death and its immediate preparation involved the presence of the priest and the administration of extreme unction and the other last rites. If many committed Protestants in the modern period became regular readers of the Bible, committed Catholics were those who took the sacramental life of the church seriously and who participated regularly in it.

THE SACRAMENTAL PRINCIPLE

The traditional Catholic emphasis on the sacraments led various commentators over the years to suggest that Catholicism is a sacramental religion, that the importance it gives to the sacramental principle is one of its most distinctive features. A sacrament always involves something concrete and visible, something like water and oil, bread and wine. When words are added to it, words evocative of the Christian mystery, it becomes an instrument of grace. To emphasize sacraments is to emphasize that God comes to us not in a purely spiritual way or simply in the inwardness of individual hearts but rather through visible and tangible things and in the context of the community. Sacraments presuppose and give expression to a certain understanding of human life. Humans are not pure spirits, nor are we spirits unfortunately exiled into bodies. We are by nature and by God's design embodied spirits. We relate to one another and to the world through our senses. In a very real sense we are our bodies.

The whole of biblical religion is in the broad sense sacramental. Israel had its Temple and its ritual and the law, which gave specific and concrete form to its daily life. In and through such things the Jewish people encountered their God and sought to do God's will. The human word is itself a kind of sacrament. In the Bible the word of Moses and of the prophets gave expression to the word of God. The scriptures have a sacramental quality in that they are God's word in visible form.

The sacramental principle is closely allied to what Christians believe about the incarnation of the Word of God in Jesus. In him the invisible and transcendent took on visible and tangible form. One of the prefaces for the liturgy of Christmas puts it this way: "In the wonder of the incarnation your eternal Word has brought to the eye of faith a new and radiant vision of your glory. In him we see our God made visible and so are caught up in the love of the God we cannot see."

In a true although somewhat analogous sense of the word, all of created reality has a sacramental character. Everything, in so far as it is made by God, reflects something of the truth, the beauty, and the life-affirming energy of God. Historically, Catholicism has manifested a certain affinity with the romantic sense of the majesty and mystery of nature. This was particularly so in German Romanticism at the beginning of the nineteenth century. It provoked a real renewal in German Catholicism. Nature mysticism was certainly not embraced for itself but was experienced as a kind of sacrament, capable of mediating a sense of the transcendent creator of nature. Some Catholics today are recognizing a comparable affinity between their religious sensitivities and contemporary concerns with ecology and with a rediscovery, beyond scientific and technological approaches, of nature as such.

If all of creation reflects something of the creator, human beings are capable of doing it in a particularly intense way. According to the Book of Genesis, humans are made in the image and likeness of God and stand in a special relationship with God. What precisely constitutes the divine image in us is difficult to say. Over the centuries religious thinkers have identified different features or aspects of human life in this regard. Many have focused on our spiritual capacities, on our mind and will. Today there is a greater appreciation that the text refers to the whole person, including body and spirit. Contemporary exegetes also point to the fact that the biblical text refers to male and female together and in doing so brings out the social nature of human life. We reflect God in our relationships with one another, and perhaps most forcefully in the fundamental relationship of man and woman. The Genesis accounts of creation in their different ways emphasize the role that human beings are called to play in collaborating with God's creative activity and in assuming stewardship for creation.

The basis in the creation narratives for a broadly sacramental understanding of human life is reinforced and deepened by the message of the New Testament. According to a traditional Catholic view of the incarnation, the entry into human life of the divine Word has implications for all of human life. In becoming incarnate in Jesus of Nazareth, the Word in some way drew close to all humans, giving them a deeper dignity and a more intimate relationship with God. In his famous parable of the last judgment in Matthew 25, Jesus says that what we do or fail to do to the poor and the sick, and more generally to those in need, we do or fail to do to him. Paul claimed at one time that in some sense he no longer lived, that it was Christ who lived in him. Nor was his sense of identification with Christ restricted to himself. He saw all of Christian life as including a form of mutual indwelling of Christ and believers. It is against the background of this kind of Christ mysticism that one has to understand his teaching about the body of Christ. We are all, though many, members of Christ and of one another. The gospel of John affirms the same basic truth in saying that Christ is the vine and that we are the branches. All believers are in Christ and, being in him, share his life.

By both nature and grace we are, and are called to be, sacraments for one another, visible signs and tangible expressions of the infinite mystery that grounds and permeates all of life. The presence of Christ's Spirit deepens in believers their sacramental quality. It enables them to be sacraments of Christ's healing, forgiving, saving, and loving presence in the world. The early Christian writer Tertullian affirmed that it was the way that Christians loved one another that attracted pagans to them.

MARY AND THE SAINTS

If one recognizes a potential sacramental quality to all of human life, it is not surprising that those people in whom that quality is thought to have been developed in a striking way should be honored and venerated and held up for emulation. Canonized or spontaneously acclaimed, saints are those women and men who are recognized as having lived the Christian life to a certain degree of perfection. Given the Catholic insistence on the necessity of grace, saints are seen as those in whom God's grace, for whatever complex of reasons, has been able to bear its fruit to an unusual degree. Francis of Assisi was widely regarded as a saint even during his lifetime. His detachment, his love of poverty, his deep devotion to the humanity of Jesus and especially to the scenes of his birth and to the dark drama of his death, led people to think of Francis as a living embodiment of what Jesus had said and done. If any saint was a sacrament of Christ, it was certainly Francis. He was able in twelfth-century Italy to provide people with an attractive and contemporary expression of authentic Christian discipleship.

What the Catholic tradition saw in Francis and in many other saints, it saw in another and deeper way in Mary, the mother of Jesus. Although over the centuries devotion to Mary has taken different forms and found different outlets, it has been a part of the Catholic world almost from the beginning. If sanctity has to do with the presence of grace and with the quality of a person's response to it, Mary is the greatest of all the saints. Basing itself primarily on the first two chapters of the gospel of Luke and on what John has to say about the marriage feast of Cana and about Mary's presence at the foot of the cross, Catholicism has seen in Mary a unique model of Christian discipleship and the highest example of the way in which God includes humanity in the process of its own salvation.

Luke's account of the annunciation stresses the way in which Mary was invited to become a part of God's saving plan. She was to do this by assenting freely and in faith to be the mother of the Messiah. Her *Fiat,* her "Here am I, the servant of the Lord; let it be with me according to your word" (Lk 1:38), represents the ideal kind of attitude that people who believe themselves called by God should have. If salvation begins with God and God's grace, it respects and uses human freedom. Our response of faith and obedience and love is essential not only for our own salvation but also as a necessary condition for the sacramental role that we are invited to play for others.

Probably most striking, especially to outsiders, about the Catholic attitude to Mary has been the rich and warm and tender devotion that it has fostered. This has found expression in a variety of forms corresponding to different periods and places. Particular emphasis has been given to the Christmas story and to the young mother giving birth in relative poverty. The great tradition of the "smiling Madonnas" has underlined the intimacy and the joy of the maternal relationship. Perhaps the greatest stress has been put on Mary's involvement in the death of her son. The well-known medieval Marian hymn *"Stabat Mater"* evokes countless paintings depicting the suffering and even tormented compassion of Mary confronted with the reality of Jesus' suffering. Some of the greatest religious paintings of the Renaissance and the Baroque periods depict the triumph of Mary. She is taken up to heaven where she is shown reigning in splendor beside the risen Christ. In Michelangelo's powerful and threatening fresco of the last judgment in the Sistine chapel, Mary is the maternal and womanly advocate, the refuge of the sinner from the wrath of the just judge.

The rosary is one of the most traditional of Catholic forms of piety. It is built on the repetition of the Hail Mary and on meditation on what are called the joyful, the sorrowful, and the glorious mysteries. These are obviously primarily the mysteries of the life of Christ, but Mary's role in them is stressed and given an added dimension by the rhythmic repetition of the prayer that so directly evokes her. One both prays to Mary and identifies with her in contemplating the life and destiny of Jesus.

Catholic dogmatic teaching about Mary is rooted in and is meant to deepen and give direction to Marian devotion. The fundamental dogma here is not primarily related to Mary at all but rather to Christ. The defense by the council of Ephesus in 431 of the title Mother of God was above all a defense of traditional faith in the ultimate identity of Jesus. The divine and the human in Jesus are so united that, as paradoxical as it sounds, one can say that the eternal God was born and that the impassable divine Word died. The Word was incapable of being born or dying as God but could do both in and through the humanity of Jesus. The intimacy of the union between the divine and the human in Jesus justifies our calling Mary the Mother of God.

The two modern Marian dogmas, the immaculate conception and the assumption, reveal as much about the meaning of salvation in Christ as they do about the special grace of which Mary was the recipient. Without grace, without God's forgiveness and help, humanity is trapped in sin. With grace, however, there is a possibility of a new and renewed life, a life that one day will be brought to its fulfillment in the resurrection of the body. The dogma of the immaculate conception affirms that Christ's saving activity embraced the totality of Mary's life beginning with the very moment of her conception. In the depths of her being she was never touched by the sin of the first humans, the so-called sin of the world, in the way that everyone else has been. In the assumption we see our own destiny. Salvation in Christ is not simply salvation of souls. It has implications for the whole of our embodied existence, implications even in some way for the whole of the cosmos. Beyond what it affirms about her destiny, the doctrine of the assumption of Mary expresses the biblical hope for a new heaven and a new earth.

THE PLACE OF ART

If Catholic sacramentalism naturally flows over into a general appreciation and veneration for saints and especially for Mary, it just as naturally seeks concrete forms to give expression to its devotion. Medieval Catholicism in particular cherished relics and made them the focus of pilgrimages and the object of deeply felt devotional practices. Churches were built in honor of the saints, and art was commissioned to recount their lives and to celebrate their present state of glory in heaven. Both Mary and the saints were regarded as powerful intercessors to whom one could turn to seek help in time of need.

In the eighth and ninth centuries Eastern Christianity was torn by what has come to be known as the iconoclastic controversy. Perhaps in reaction to what they considered to be abuses, emperors and bishops rejected the growing practice of veneration of icons and, in the name of the biblical prohibition of images for God, unleashed a wave of considerable destructiveness. In 787 at the seventh ecumenical council (Nicaea II), iconoclasm was formally rejected and the use and the veneration of images in Christian devotion was affirmed to be a part of orthodox faith. The traditional practice was justified by an appeal to the incarnation in which the invisible God had taken on human form. The fact that Christ himself is the true image or icon of God gives a christological basis for the development of Christian art. Icons of Christ and of the saints extend the incarnational principle and answer to a deeply felt human need for a visible focus for devotion. The theology of icons that developed in Eastern Christianity emphasized their quasi-sacramental character. In the West the emphasis was put more on the fact that veneration was not directed to the symbolism of the work of art but to the person that it represented. The West also tended to underline religious art's didactic function.

The Protestant Reformation brought in its wake a fresh wave of iconoclasm in various parts of western and central

Europe. In the eyes of some of the reformers, the proliferation in the churches of paintings and statues distracted people from the simple and fundamental truths and realities that were meant to be at the heart of their religious life. Images of Mary and of the saints in particular seemed to smack of idolatry, the worship of the creature in place of the creator.

The arts in all their forms have been at home in the Catholic tradition for most of its history. Paintings, sculptures, and such things as illuminated manuscripts were appreciated for their ability to give visible form to and to communicate religious truths. Depictions of the passion, for example, brought home in a powerful but accessible way for illiterate people the story of Jesus' suffering and death and its meaning for them. The stained-glass windows of the great cathedrals with their cycles of stories and texts from the Old and the New Testaments have been called the comic books of the Middle Ages. They enabled countless generations of believers, unable to read the scriptures, to come into contact with their content and to do so in ways that caught and deeply impressed their imaginations.

Initially Christians met for the liturgy in private homes and then in houses that were set aside and slightly altered for the liturgical needs of the community. With the Constantinian peace and with the support of the emperor and wealthy converts, church architecture began to be developed. In some cases the buildings themselves were remarkable structures that reflected something of the majesty of God and of the seriousness of the religious activities that were to take place in them.

Christian churches, unlike pagan temples, were not conceived of as dwelling places of the divinity but rather as structures within which the community of faith could gather and carry out its liturgical life. With time these buildings began to be decorated with mosaics and wall paintings and statues and eventually with splendid colored windows. All these things helped to create an atmosphere in which the building itself was able to foster a religious sensitivity and a religious attitude. Obviously, individual churches did this in different ways. Sometimes the religious purpose of such efforts was lost sight of. Some churches were so large and richly decorated that they revealed more about the wealth and power of local ecclesiastical and political leaders than about the spiritual nature of the activities the buildings were meant to house.

Music has always been felt to be a form of art particularly suitable for worship. As with the other arts, it too has taken on a variety of forms in the course of history. Some of these included the whole congregation, while others were reserved to individual cantors. With the rise of the more complex types of music associated with polyphony, choirs and instruments took on more important roles.

As positively as the Catholic tradition has regarded the role of the arts in religion in general and more particularly as complementing church architecture and as providing appropriate forms and a suitable context for the liturgy, individual Catholics on occasion have risen up against what they have considered to be abuses in this area. Religion is more than an aesthetic experience. Art that attracts too much attention to itself can distract worshipers from what they are supposed to be about. In spite of the real possibility of abuse, however, the commitment of Catholics to the sacramental principle has disposed them to seek in the arts a help and support for the fostering and strengthening of faith and of corporate religious life.

RETHINKING SACRAMENTAL THEOLOGY

In the period leading up to Vatican II, the word *sacrament,* for most Catholics, referred almost exclusively to the traditional seven sacraments. As different among themselves as baptism and confession, marriage and extreme unction were, they were all understood to belong to the single category of sacrament. According to one of the well-known catechetical definitions, "a sacrament is an outward sign instituted by Christ to give grace." The tendency was to think of sacraments somewhat in isolation from the broader life of the church. They were ritual actions performed usually by priests through which God granted grace to people in different moments and in various situations of their lives.

Given this background, many Catholics were surprised to learn that Vatican II in a number of its documents spoke of the church as a sacrament. Some asked: Is the council affirming that the church is, as it were, an eighth sacrament, or does the word when applied to the church mean something quite different? The *Dogmatic Constitution on the Church* suggested an answer when it explained that the church is "a sign and instrument...of communion with God and of unity among all [people]" (no. 1). Two traditional ideas about sacraments—that they are signs that point to something beyond themselves, and that they are means and instruments by which God's grace is communicated—are picked up here and applied to the church as such. The whole life of the church and not just its liturgical activity has a sacramental character. It is a visible sign of the invisible presence in the world of God's grace and in some way an instrument that God uses in calling people into communion with him.

As novel as this way of thinking about the church at first sight appeared, it was, like so much else at Vatican II, quite traditional. The application of sacramental language to the church was quite common in the patristic period and had only slowly over the centuries disappeared from Catholic consciousness.

The background for the use of the term in the early church is provided by passages like Ephesians 1:3–10 and 3:1–13 and Colossians, 1:24–29. The focus in these texts is on the theme of *mystery,* something hidden or unknown. In this case it refers to God's plan of salvation hidden from all eternity but now made manifest in Christ. Both letters affirm that Christ is the divine mystery in human form. Now that Christ is no longer visibly present in himself in the world, his mission and function in this regard continue to some degree in the life of the church. The mystery is now Christ in the community of the faithful. The Greek word for mystery is *mysterion.* In an early Latin version of the New Testament, it was translated as *sacramentum.* This simple fact provides a key for beginning to understand what Vatican II, following so many patristic bishops and theologians, intended in calling the church a sacrament. Christ is the fundamental sacrament, the sacrament par excellence. To say this is simply to say in another way what is affirmed by the doctrine of the incarnation. In Jesus the eternal and invisible Word of God took on human form and in doing so revealed the hidden divine mystery. In his person, teaching, life, and destiny, Jesus not only makes God visible, but he is an instrument, a means through which God's offer of forgiveness and life is brought into the midst of human history. Jesus is the sacrament of God. This is expressed in John's gospel when Jesus says: "Who sees me sees the Father."

If Jesus is the primordial sacrament, the church which is his body, the community of faith animated by his Spirit, is and is called to be a sign and instrument of him and of the salvation that he came to bring. The word *economy* in the New Testament refers to God's plan of salvation. It is an incarnational, a sacramental economy. Just as God came to us in and through the concrete human reality of Jesus, so God's revelation and grace continue to be present in the world in a visible and tangible form in and through the community of faith. The church in all aspects of its life and activity is a sacrament of Christ and of Christ's Spirit, a sign and instrument of their saving, healing, life-giving activity.

The formal endorsement by Vatican II of the notion of the sacramental nature of the church presents an opportunity for broadening and deepening our appreciation of what is entailed in the traditional understanding of Catholicism as a sacramental religion. One area in which this has been done in the post-conciliar period has been in regard to the relation of the church to the vast non-Christian world that surrounds it. Vatican II reflects what might be called an optimism of grace. It affirms that in spite of sin God never has abandoned humanity but has stayed close to it and in various ways offered people the possibility of salvation. With the coming of Christ, God's saving activity is focused in a particular way on the church, but it is by no means restricted to it. God wills the salvation of all and, in ways unknown to us, remains present to people everywhere, offering them a share in the divine life. Karl Rahner spoke of God's universal offer of salvation. For him every human life is lived out in relationship to the God of grace, even though because of their religious and cultural backgrounds many are unable to recognize that this is the deepest meaning of their experience. To speak of the church as a sacrament in this context is to point to its role within a world where grace, at least as offer, is universal. In the midst of that world, the church proclaims and celebrates in explicit language what in a more hidden way God does throughout the length and breadth of human history.

If the church itself, in dependence on Christ as the primordial sacrament, is the fundamental sacrament, then this suggests a new way of thinking about the seven sacraments. They represent intense and significant moments in the life of the church, moments when it draws itself together and focuses its sacramental nature on particular individuals or on a particular community. The seven sacraments are acts of both the risen Christ and of the church. Through them Christ encounters individual believers, but he does so within the context of the community. Every sacrament in some way involves the whole community and has an effect on it. The relationship with God that is mediated through the sacraments entails a modification of a person's relationship to the community of faith. An example of what is implied here is the renewed awareness that many have today that baptism is not simply a means for taking away original sin and communicating grace. It is a key moment in a larger rite of initiation by which a person becomes a member of the church. Receiving a share in the saving gift of Christ is inseparable from becoming a member of Christ's body. The ecclesial dimension of baptism is obvious and to some degree has always been understood. What the renewed emphasis on the church as sacrament has done is to bring out this traditional truth in a new and more forceful way.

LITURGY AND SACRAMENTS

The notion of the church as a sacrament and the related concept of the ecclesial nature of the seven sacraments helped to reinforce, and were in turn given concrete form by, the liturgical renewal that was taking place in the Catholic Church throughout the first half of the twentieth century. Vatican II endorsed the work of the liturgical movement in its broad outlines and called for its further implementation. This was to be achieved above all by a general renewal of all liturgical and sacramental rites.

For centuries Catholic theology tended to study the sacraments in isolation from the liturgy. It focused on them as instruments or causes of grace and tried to determine how and why they were effective and what minimal requirements had to be met for them to be valid. For neo-Scholastic theology, the dominant theological approach in the church between c. 1850 and 1950, the liturgy was something secondary. It provided a context of ritual and prayer within which the sacramental actions took place. Not required for their validity, it could easily be reduced to a minimum or dispensed with entirely in cases of necessity.

Among the more important contributions over the last quarter of a century of North American theology to the self-understanding of Catholicism has been its insistence on the need to resituate sacramental theology within the context of a theology of the liturgy. The liturgy is the more fundamental and all-embracing reality of which the sacraments are to be understood as key elements.

Both subjectively and objectively the liturgy is at the heart of Catholic identity. Subjectively, it is through participation in the liturgy—participation in the weekly eucharist, in baptisms and weddings and funerals, in celebrations of reconciliation and of the anointing of the sick, and in exposure to the regular rhythm of the liturgical year—that most Catholics are socialized into the community of faith. Here Catholic values and attitudes are spoken about and celebrated and experienced in symbolic and ritual forms. The liturgical renewal called for by the council has had as one of its chief ends to facilitate the active involvement in the liturgy of all believers. In order to do this, the rites were simplified and above all put into the vernacular. In the increasingly pluralistic and secular environment in which most North American Catholics live, the liturgy has become more crucial for communicating and reinforcing Catholic identity than ever before.

The subjective significance of the liturgy for individual Catholics and for Catholic communities in deepening their sense of belonging to the church is rooted ultimately in its objective nature as a privileged expression of church life. A traditional saying related the rule of faith to the rule of prayer *(lex orandi, lex credendi)*. In the liturgy the church expresses itself and its faith with special intensity and clarity. In the liturgy we offer praise and worship to the God who has turned to us in Christ and who continues to be present among us through the Spirit, we recall and celebrate and render present the saving mystery of Christ's death and resurrection, we become conscious of ourselves as a community of faith, we are challenged to live the values of the kingdom in our lives, and we look forward in hope to final fulfillment. The different moments of the church year, the various sacraments and devotions, bring out different aspects of the gospel message and of what concretely is involved in Christian discipleship.

The word liturgy comes from the Greek *leitourgia,* which in turn is made up of two words, *laos* (people) and *ergon* (work). The liturgy is a work of the people, an act of the whole community. It is the public, official prayer of the church. Unlike private prayer and devotion, it is a corporate act and follows more or less fixed forms established by church authority. At a deeper level it is an act of the whole Christ, of the risen Christ and of his body, the church. When we gather for the liturgy, we become aware of ourselves as a community of faith united with Christ and animated by his Spirit. We are caught up as it were into the heavenly liturgy that Christ continues to offer to the Father. All liturgy is marked by a double movement: from God to us, and from us to God. Through Christ and in the Spirit, God communicates something of the divine life, perhaps in the form of faith or trust, of courage or love; we, for our part, inspired by the Spirit and united with Christ, offer worship, praise, and thanksgiving. We pray for God's continuing help and blessing for ourselves and for the world.

Sacraments are part of the liturgy and in fact constitute its high points. They should not, therefore, be thought of in isolation or simply as means by which God bestows grace on us. They are liturgical actions and as such are acts not just of the priest but of the whole gathered community; they involve worship and prayer as well as the conferring of grace. As part of the liturgy they need to be celebrated in ways that bring out their symbolism and that enable the community as a whole to participate actively in them. Liturgical symbols should be able to speak with a certain eloquence. Early Christian baptism was accomplished not by sprinkling a few drops of water on a person's forehead but by immersion in a real bath or font. The going down into the font expressed in the most concrete of ways Paul's understanding of baptism as a descent into the tomb with Christ so that one might rise up with him to newness of life.

The rituals developed in the post-conciliar period, whatever minor inadequacies they might have, represent an extraordinary gift to all Catholics. They bring out in a way that has not been the case for centuries the ecclesial implications of the various sacraments.

The new rite of Christian initiation for adults (RCIA), originally requested by missionary bishops, has found a remarkably enthusiastic reception in many North American parishes. It is rooted in the catechumenate that was developed in the early church as a way of ensuring that adult converts would have the opportunity to develop not only the understanding but also the moral and spiritual attitudes required for a mature baptismal commitment. The new RCIA underlines the community dimension of what is taking place. It unfolds in a group setting and involves baptized members of the community as sponsors of the individual catechumens. The various stages of their journey are marked by ritual actions that take place within the Sunday liturgy of the welcoming parish. The whole process culminates with their receiving all three sacraments of initiation—baptism, confirmation, and the eucharist—within a community liturgy, preferably at the Easter Vigil.

Becoming a Catholic Christian is not something that takes place simply between the individual and God or even between the individual and a priest representing God. It concerns in a variety of ways a concrete faith community. Baptism is part of a rite of initiation into the church. The RCIA helps catechumens to be aware of, and to reflect on, the ecclesial dimension of their decision. Not only that, members of the community are invited to accompany potential converts as they prepare themselves to receive the sacrament. The fact that certain rites that are a part of the process are celebrated in the larger community reminds all believers who they are as members of the church and the rights and responsibilities that belong to them as a result. A well-planned and well-executed RCIA program can be an effective means not only of preparing potential converts for church membership but of renewing and deepening a parish's sense of itself.

In one form or another, the eucharist or the Mass has always been at the center of Catholic life. Since the medieval period one of the precepts or laws of the church has required attendance at Mass on Sundays and holy days under pain of sin. Catholics, moreover, have not only gone to Mass, they have often had it celebrated for their intentions and especially for deceased friends and relatives. In recent centuries the Mass was probably seen more as something that priests offered for people than something that the laity themselves were expected to be actively involved in, but even then it remained the central religious and ritual action of corporate Catholic life.

The recent renewal of the eucharistic liturgy had as its major purpose to facilitate people's understanding of it and participation in it. The eucharist clearly constitutes the center of the liturgical life of the church. Everything else leads to it or flows from it. Like the rest of the liturgy, but even more obviously than some parts of it, it is a community action. A group of believers gathers with their priest and with and in Christ and through the Spirit they offer praise and worship to God, listen to the scriptures, make memory of what Jesus said and did at the last supper and in doing so render present the power for life of his death and resurrection. Through communion individual believers are united with Christ in his self-giving love and with one another. The particular grace of the eucharist, Thomas Aquinas and much of the tradition before him taught, is the charity or love that binds believers together. It is not by chance that both the eucharist and the church are called the body of Christ. At least part of the reason for the church's existence is that it might celebrate the eucharist; a chief purpose of the eucharist on the other hand is to build up the church so that it might more and more become the body of Christ. The body of Christ that is the eucharist and the body of Christ that is the church are inseparable.

The possibility that the new rites provide for a community celebration of the sacrament of penance or reconciliation, even when it is accompanied by individual confession, brings out the ecclesial nature of this sacrament as well. Our sins have implications for others as theirs do for us. There is a natural solidarity among human beings, a solidarity that is simply rendered more intense within the community of faith. The ongoing conversion of a person or of a community cannot help but have an effect on other individuals and communities as well. The communal forms of penance bring out the role that the church as church plays in the process of both conversion and forgiveness. God's forgiveness does not leave us in our isolation but rather draws us into a closer bond with the community of faith. Forgiveness in the early centuries was identified with the *pax ecclesiae,* with the reestablishment through the bishop of reconciliation and peace with the church.

The rediscovery of the ecclesial dimension of the sacraments has opened up new possibilities in other areas as well. The revised ritual for the anointing of the sick can serve here as a final example. As in the case of all the other sacraments, this one too is an act of the church; it is not simply something that is offered to isolated individuals. Ideally it should involve a community, whether it be large or small. The practice of celebrating the sacrament of the sick within the context of the eucharist and of doing both within a setting that includes family and friends opens up rich possibilities for pastoral service and for renewing the Catholic identity of all concerned.

The sacrament of the sick in itself reflects the general sacramental nature of Catholic life. The tradition has always recognized the spiritual as well as human importance of the challenge of serious illness and above all of the threat of death. Such situations touch people both in the center of their identity and in the way they see others relating to them. The concreteness of oil and touch and ritual prayer can sometimes reach people in such states when nothing else can. The new rites do this more effectively than the older ones and add at the same time a heightened sense of the social implications of what is taking place. The community of faith as such reaches out to the sick and the dying and affirms that they are still members of it. It wants to be with them and help them in any way that it can. These desires take on concrete form in the presence of family and friends. They share in the suffering and offer their prayers and support. The ecclesial nature of the sacrament invites believers to become involved with and supportive of those in the community who are confronted with illness and death.

WORD AND SACRAMENT

The present chapter began with a reference to an older tendency to contrast Protestant and Catholic forms of Christianity in terms of their respective emphasis on word or sacrament. Whatever truth that contrast might once have had, differences in this area are currently being overcome. Many Protestants have become enthusiastic about the liturgical movement that has so transformed Catholic experience, and Catholics since Vatican II have been growing in their appreciation of the role of the scriptures in their religious life, and especially in the liturgy.

The word enters into the sacramental life of the church in two distinct forms, the most obvious being the scriptures. The other way in which the word is important is the role that it plays within the sacramental ritual itself. Sacraments involve material things like bread and wine, oil and water, things that by their very nature already suggest some kind of meaning. To share food with others especially in certain contexts often suggests a desire to enter into real contact, into communion, with them. In a religious setting that sharing is rooted in and given added meaning by a sense of God's presence in the act.

What makes the eucharist a sacrament and the heart of Catholic liturgical life is not simply the bread and the wine that are used in it, nor the fact that they are shared. To the material elements and the gesture of their sharing one needs to add the words that give the ritual its distinctive meaning. The repetition of what Jesus said over the bread and the wine at the last supper gives the eucharist its Christian character: This is my body, my very being given for you; this is my life-blood poured out for the forgiveness of sins. More than just the human sharing of food, the eucharist is the self-giving of the Word incarnate. Christ loved us and gave himself for us. That self-giving embraced all of his life and was brought to a climax on the cross. It is this that is rendered present in the eucharist and this, too, with which believers are invited to become united through communion. The community that is rooted in and marked by the eucharist is the body of Christ, a community at the heart of whose life is his self-giving love.

St. Augustine once described the role of the liturgical presider in relation to the community as being that of breaking the bread of the word as well as breaking the bread of the eucharist. Word and sacrament belong together. The scriptures are central to Christian life and especially to the liturgy. This was a truth that Vatican II emphasized repeatedly and that it tried to serve in a number of its concrete recommendations. The council strongly urged that the administration of every sacrament include scripture readings and a word of clarification. Scripture plays a particularly important role in the eucharist. The new lectionary contains three readings for Sundays in place of the earlier two and, more important, offers a three-year cycle where before the same readings were read every year. This means that Catholics who attend the weekly eucharist are exposed to a larger selection of biblical texts than ever before. Echoing a concern of the Protestant Reformation, Vatican II insisted on the importance of preaching and especially on the importance of the biblical homily. The latter phrase refers to preaching that is rooted in the actual liturgical celebration and in its biblical texts and that takes as its goal the relating of their content to the life and experience of the gathered community.

The council's document on revelation affirms that the scriptures should constitute the heart and soul of Catholic theology and should be a major source for the spiritual life. Other documents having to do with the ministry of priests and bishops insist that preaching and teaching are their first responsibility. All these developments are helping Catholics to rediscover the complementarity of word and sacrament that marked the experience of the early church. The word itself has a sacramental quality. Through the human word of scripture we encounter the word of God. In an analogous sense the human word of the preacher, when he preaches the gospel, gives voice in the here and now to the word of Christ. On the other hand, sacraments are like words that have taken on visible form. In a striking phrase St. Paul declared that when we celebrate the eucharist we "proclaim the Lord's death" (1 Cor 11:26). Symbol and ritual, especially within the context of a well-celebrated liturgy, can speak with a power that is often denied to the word alone.

COMMUNITY, HISTORY, AND FAITH

What has been said in this chapter about sacraments and liturgy has reinforced and to some degree made more concrete what was affirmed in earlier chapters about the centrality to Catholicism of community, history, and faith. By definition, the liturgy is a communal action. It is not something that one ordinarily does by oneself and certainly not in one's own name. It presupposes membership in the church and a willingness to gather with other church members in order to pray and worship and to open up to the gifts that God offers through the various sacraments. The eucharist, in particular, we saw, is at the heart of the life of the faith community. It expresses the nature of the bond that unites believers even as it deepens and reinforces it. For the vast majority of Catholics it is the ordinary way to experience membership in the church and gain some insight into its implications. The challenge here is to ensure that people really experience in eucharistic celebrations that they are part of a community of faith and not isolated believers. Here what the ritual affirms presupposes and calls out for a community experience that goes beyond the boundaries of the church building. It is only to the degree that people share in such a community that they are able to experience in any kind of authentic way the communal dimension of their worship. The more real, on the other hand, the latter becomes for them, the more their sense of belonging to a community of faith will be deepened. Here as elsewhere, liturgy and life are meant to have a reciprocal influence on each other.

There are two ways in which history is a central dimension of the liturgy. In the first place, liturgy, like all effective ritual, is rooted in and reflects the history of the community that celebrates it. Liturgical change is rarely easy; the creation more or less from nothing of new liturgies is all but impossible. A major principle in the renewal called for by Vatican II was that it should be rooted in history. It should try to eliminate false or one-sided developments that had taken place over time and return to what were considered to be the more authentic forms; namely, those that had been followed in the early church. As new as such things as communion in the hand, Mass facing the people, the use of the vernacular, the access of the laity to the chalice, an emphasis on the scriptures and on preaching, and the RCIA seemed, they all represented an effort to return to earlier practice, one that those responsible for the renewal believed would facilitate the active involvement of all believers in the liturgy.

The liturgy remains a major witness to what Catholics refer to as tradition. In it one can discern much that is central to the distinctively Catholic understanding and practice of Christianity. At the same time, as the recent liturgical renewal has made clear, the liturgy requires a certain process of adaptation or incultura-tion so that it can truly be the liturgy of different periods and cultures. The challenge here as in regard to doctrine is to find the right balance between the past and the present, between the abiding substance of the liturgy and the forms that can and should be changed in a new cultural context.

The liturgy relates to history in a second and more mysteri-ous way. Central to all liturgy is the notion of *anamnesis*, which literally means "memorial" or "memory." In the eucharist we make memory of the death and resurrection of Jesus and of his future coming. What is intended here is more than mere remem-brance. In the biblical sense of the word, memorial suggests a rendering present of a past event so that new generations can encounter its power for life and salvation. That such a thing was possible was the conviction that gave the Jewish celebration of the Passover its unique value. The same conviction lies at the heart of the Christian liturgy.

All of the liturgy and not just the eucharist is in some sense an *anamnesis*, a memorial of the paschal mystery. In every sacra-mental act the death and resurrection of Jesus and their power for forgiveness and new life are rendered present in the liturgical assembly and brought to bear on its life and especially on the lives of those individuals to whom the act is particularly directed. The *anamnesis* of the liturgy is complemented by an *epiclesis*, a prayer to God to send the Holy Spirit on the action so that it will have the effect of which it is capable. The *epiclesis* underlines the present dimension of the liturgy. We remember the past so that what Christ accomplished in it will transform us here and now and stimulate us to a life of true discipleship. The liturgy, like the scriptures, reminds us again and again that the fulfillment of God's kingdom still lies before us and that we are called to help prepare its coming.

As natural as forms of community ritual are, the Christian liturgy in what is most distinctive about it depends on faith. The sacraments presuppose faith and are meant to help strengthen and renew it. The most fundamental presupposition for the baptism of adults is that they have arrived at a certain level of explicit faith. Without faith baptism would be a relatively empty gesture. The level of our sharing in any of the sacraments depends to a considerable degree on the level of our faith. One of the major results, on the other hand, of any genuine participation in the liturgy, whether on the part of individuals or of a community, is a deepening of the life of faith.

That the liturgy proclaims the content of Christian faith in a quite special way has been a conviction of theologians and preachers from the earliest times. It would not be difficult to find in the liturgy and especially in the eucharist all the main themes of Christian revelation. Here again the subjective response of faith encounters and is nourished by its objective content.

The liturgy in the Catholic tradition reserves a special place for ordained ministers. Even if it is an act of the whole community, they have a special role to play in it. What precisely that role is will be one of the questions to be addressed in the next chapter. What should be clear from the present chapter is that the sacramental emphasis in Catholicism has influenced much that is distinctive in its life and that the recent renewal of the liturgy has broadened and deepened the ways in which the sacramental principle continues to be at work within it.

CHAPTER FIVE

A Structured Community

To Catholics and non-Catholics alike, one of the most obvious features of Catholicism is the considerable emphasis it puts on the ordained ministry, on the role of pope, bishops, priests, and deacons. Perhaps less well known to the average Catholic, but extremely important nonetheless, has been the place given in the Catholic tradition to canon law, a code of church rules and regulations that spell out among other things the precise duties and responsibilities of those in positions of leadership and the attitudes that should mark the faithful in their regard.

A traditional term that Catholics have used for the various levels of church offices is *hierarchy*. Its Greek root suggests a form of sacred leadership, a sacral or holy order of offices related in a descending pattern of importance. The word itself is not found in the New Testament but seems rather to have entered the Christian vocabulary primarily through the influence of a fifth-century anonymous Christian writer known as the Pseudo-Dionysius. Steeped in the emanationist philosophy of neo-Platonism, he conceived of the heavenly world as marked by a hierarchical ordering of the various choirs of angels. He saw the church with its different offices of relative importance descending from bishops and presbyters through deacons, lectors, and exorcists to lay people as reflecting its heavenly model.

In the Catholic tradition the language of hierarchy evokes a number of different although related elements or ideas. The one perhaps most closely associated in the minds of many with the word *hierarchy* is authority or power. The hierarchy in this case tends to be identified with the pope and the bishops. They have the authority to make decisions in the church; they have the power to determine church teaching and church law. Popes approve liturgical rituals and decide on such issues as the celibacy of the clergy, the canonization of a saint, the conditions for a valid marriage, and whether or not a theological opinion can be formally accepted as part of Catholic teaching.

The hierarchy or, perhaps better in this case, the ordained ministry is also understood to be part of the sacramental system of the church. Ordination to the episcopacy, priesthood, or diaconate is a sacrament, one of the traditional seven sacraments. In virtue of ordination priests, for example, are able to preside at the eucharist, to offer the sacrifice of the Mass. They are also the ordinary ministers of the sacraments of reconciliation and of the anointing of the sick. Just as Catholic Christianity has underlined the place of the sacraments in the Christian life, so has it stressed the indispensable role that priests are called to play in their administration. Bishops, on the other hand, are able to do sacramentally all that priests can do and in addition are regarded as the "original" ministers of confirmation. They also ordain priests and bishops. In regard to the sacraments, the pope is like other bishops. It is in fact precisely as the bishop of Rome that he exercises the particular leadership over the whole church that has come to be known as the papacy or the papal office.

In sharp contrast to the Protestant tradition, Catholicism, as also Eastern Orthodoxy, has emphasized the priestly nature of the ordained ministry. This applies to bishops as well as to those who are popularly identified as priests. The episcopacy is often identified in the Catholic tradition as the fullness of the priesthood. This language has clearly been influenced by the example of the Levitical priesthood of the Old Testament and has tended to reinforce the distinction and the separation between the ordained and the non-ordained. In the period leading up to Vatican II people often contrasted Protestant and Catholic attitudes in this area by saying that Protestant churches had ministers while Catholicism had priests.

The centrality to Catholicism of hierarchy taken in this broad sense is so obvious that one might ask whether a book dealing with distinctive features of the Catholic experience of Christianity should not have begun with it. As reasonable from one point of view as that might seem, it would have the unfortunate effect of distorting the precise role and therefore the meaning of the ordained ministry. Pope, bishops, priests, and deacons do not exist for themselves. They are not in any sense self-justifying. They exist in order to fulfill certain tasks and responsibilities related to the building up of the church, the maintaining of its unity, the deepening of its common life. Because the Christian community is a community of faith, the ordained ministry serves it first of all through preaching and teaching. It guards and hands on the gospel message and tries to relate it in positive and creative ways to changing situations. Because the community is a sacramental community, the ordained ministry presides at the liturgical actions that are so central to its common life and tries to facilitate the involvement of all the faithful in them. The hierarchy is thus in reality a service, a service to God and Christ, a service to the community and to the individuals that make it up. To bring out this element of service, the tendency at the present is increasingly to substitute the language of ministry for that of hierarchy. It has the advantage of being a biblical term and one that takes us to the heart of the life and mission of Jesus.

HIERARCHY AS MINISTRY

Words like *ministry* and *minister* are rooted in the very similar Latin words *ministerium, minister,* and *ministrare.* They suggest various forms of service or assistance. One can hear something of their original meaning in the way some countries use the language of ministry for government officials and government offices. The prime minister heads a cabinet made up of a number of other minsters responsible for various areas of government. These areas themselves are referred to as the ministry of education, the ministry of health and welfare, and so on. As analogous as this use of the language of ministry is to its use in the church, there is a difference that needs to be kept in mind. Ministry in the Christian tradition received a quite distinctive meaning because of the use that St. Jerome made of *ministerium* and *minister* in his Latin translation of the New Testament. He used these words to translate the Greek words *diakonia* and *diakonos,* words which in ordinary Greek simply meant "service" and "servant" but which in the New Testament took on special connotations because of the way that the gospel writers related them to Jesus.

There is a saying of Jesus' that comes back six times in one form or another in the three synoptic gospels. In a parallel text in Mark and Matthew it reads: "Whoever wishes to become great among you must be your servant *(diakonos)*, and whoever wishes to be first among you must be slave of all" (Mk 10:43–44; cf. Mt 20:26–27). Luke takes the same saying, modifies it somewhat, and places it in the context of the last supper. In doing so he heightens its meaning and above all underlines its importance for church structure.

Immediately after his account of what Jesus said and did in regard to the bread and wine, Luke tells us that the apostles began to dispute among themselves "which one of them was to be regarded as the greatest" (Lk 22:24). In entrusting the eucharist to them, Jesus had just offered the twelve not only the gift of himself but the key to the meaning of his life as well. This is my body, my person, given for you; this is my life blood poured out for your salvation. In a type of last will and testament Jesus both reveals the secret of his life and delivers its power for forgiveness and renewal into the hands of the disciples. The eucharist is to be at the heart of the community life that is to continue after his death. Unfortunately all they can think of is their own relative importance. The contrast between their attitude and that of Jesus could hardly be more dramatic. Their concerns, Jesus says, reflect the concerns of the rich and the powerful. They want to "lord it over" others and to have special titles used in addressing them. As common as such an attitude is in the world, Jesus says, it is not to exist among his disciples; "rather the greatest among you must become like the younger, and the leader like one who serves." He then goes on to point to the paradox of his own behavior. "For who is greater," he asks, "the one who is at the table or the one who serves? Is it not the one at the table? But I am among you as one who serves" (Lk 22:25–27).

Although Luke has no account of any washing of the disciples' feet, what he has Jesus say here corresponds perfectly to the scene in John's gospel where it is described. Although the reference there is more clearly to Jesus' coming death and its cleansing power, the fact that he assumes the role of the servant is self-evident. He who is the Lord and teacher washes his disciples' feet and in doing so teaches them that they should do the same thing for one another (Jn 13:3–16). Mark's gospel sums us both of these incidents in a single, telling phrase: "The Son of Man came not to be served but to serve, and to give his life a ransom for many" (Mk 10:45).

Jesus is the *diakonos,* the servant, the minister *par excellence.* His whole life is a service rendered to God and to human beings. Although including his life and preaching, his ministry reaches its climax in the fidelity and love that bring him to the cross. It is all this that gives *ministry*–service–its special meaning in the Christian tradition. It is rooted in the life and self-giving of Jesus. To understand ministry in a Christian context one has to relate it to Christ and to the ministry that defined and gave meaning to his life and death.

The first Christians were clearly conscious of the special overtones that the word *diakonia* had for their faith. They recognized in it an attitude and a practice that were to mark the life of every disciple of Jesus. Matthew 25 in its account of the last judgment affirms that we will be judged according to whether we have ministered to people in need, whether we have served the sick, the homeless, and the naked.

If *diakonia* was to be a feature of all Christian life, the same word was widely used in the Christian scriptures to describe what later would be called church office or hierarchy. This is already quite explicit in Luke's account of the last supper. There Jesus refers to those who want to be leaders. To be a leader in the Christian community is to accept a responsibility of service, of ministry. It is something that is rooted in and should reflect the ministry of Jesus himself.

To think of hierarchy in terms of ministry is not to deny either the authority or the responsibility of officeholders. It is rather to point to the basic attitude that such persons should have and to the fact that who and what they are is not self-justifying. Church ministers exist to be instruments of Christ and the Spirit and to serve the community of faith.

THE APOSTOLIC MINISTRY

The word *ministry,* by itself, does not define the precise nature of church leadership, nor does it suggest the kind of responsibilities it entails. For these things one has to look more closely at what church ministers in the New Testament period and later actually did. A key term in filling out an understanding of the Christian ministry is *apostle.* The Nicene Creed proclaims faith in "one, holy, catholic, and apostolic church." We have already suggested in chapter 3 something of the importance of the related notions of apostolic tradition and apostolic succession.

The Greek word for apostle, *apostolos,* is a passive form of the verb "to send." An apostle is someone who is sent from someone to someone else, someone therefore who represents another. Although the gospels occasionally identify the twelve in the life of Jesus as apostles, the general consensus of biblical scholars is that the word *apostle* is associated in a special way with the experience of the resurrection. In spite of some skeptics, the fact that Jesus, during his earthly ministry, chose from among his disciples a group of twelve seems fairly certain. The number points to the group's meaning. It evokes the twelve tribes of Israel. Although the tribes had become dispersed over the course of history, a part of Jewish hope for the end times was that they would be reestablished. In associating a group of twelve with him, Jesus seems to have been making a statement about the significance of his life and ministry. The twelve either represented the beginning of the reestablishment of the twelve tribes for the coming end times or were a promise that such a reestablishment would soon take place. Although the twelve continued to play an important role in the early Jerusalem community, the apostolic ministry gradually assumed a more dominant place in the growing understanding of the church. The resurrection experiences were church-founding. Through them the apostles received the commission to preach the gospel and to gather believers into a community of faith.

As fundamental as the category of apostle was for the early church, it seems to have been understood in a variety of ways. There was a broad sense of the term that was used to describe "apostles" of local churches, messengers, and representatives chosen and sent from one community to another. The more technical use of the term was related to the resurrection. Luke, as noted above, tended to identify the twelve with the apostles and saw them providing a historical link between the time of Jesus and that of the church. Paul, in the face of fairly biting opposition, insisted that he too was an apostle even though he had never known the earthly Jesus. His apostolate was rooted in his conversion experience, an experience that he saw as analogous to the resurrection appearances to the other apostles, and in his being commissioned by the risen Christ to preach the gospel. He came to see his own apostolic work as directed to the Gentiles as Peter's was to the Jews.

That Paul played an extraordinary role in the development of the church is a simple fact of history, a fact reflected in his own extensive writings and also in the way his missionary activities are recounted in the Acts of the Apostles. The fact that a number of the later books of the New Testament, including those addressed to Timothy and Titus, were attributed to Paul simply underlines the continuing importance that his ministry and teaching were recognized as having. Ephesians speaks of the church as "built upon the foundation of the apostles and prophets" (Eph 2:20), and the Book of Revelation describes a vision of the holy city Jerusalem descending at the end of time from heaven, "And the wall of the city has twelve foundations, and on them are the twelve names of the twelve apostles of the Lamb" (Rv 21:14).

The significance attributed by the first generations of Christians to the apostles and to the continuing connection of the church with them comes out in a number of ways. We have already referred to the development of the ideas of apostolic succession and apostolic tradition. The same concern is shown in the process of sorting out which books belonged to the canon of the New Testament. The four gospels were accepted because Matthew and John were believed to be written by apostles, Luke was thought to have been a companion of Paul, and Mark was considered a disciple and secretary of Peter. There is an ancient legend that before leaving Jerusalem on their missionary journeys the twelve apostles gathered together and one after the other affirmed the various articles that make up the Apostles' Creed. As legendary as the account is, it eloquently underlines just how important for early Christianity its connection to the faith and life of the apostles remained.

THE DEVELOPMENT OF CATHOLIC STRUCTURE

There is no indication that Jesus spelled out in any detail how the local communities founded by the preaching of the apostles were to be structured. The apostles themselves did not seem to have any clear pattern that they followed. The impression one has from the New Testament as a whole is that church structure developed in the course of the first generations and that it only began to take on the classical Catholic pattern at the end of the New Testament period.

There is a passage in the early part of the Acts of the Apostles (6:1–6) that offers an insight into how local church structure developed. As the community expanded, Jewish Christians of Greek background complained to the twelve that in comparison with Christians of Hebrew background their widows and orphans were not receiving a fair share of the charitable support of the community. Having gathered together the whole community, the twelve announced that because of their responsibilities for preaching and teaching they were unable themselves to look after all the other needs that were arising. They therefore asked that seven capable people be chosen and assigned to look after the problem. Once the community chose the seven, "they had these men stand before the apostles, who prayed and laid their hands on them" (Acts 6:6).

Because of a reference in the text to a waiting on tables *(diakonizein)*, later generations came to interpret the incident as marking the appointment of the first deacons. From what we see Stephen and some of the others subsequently doing, however, it seems that they were appointed as leaders of the Greek-speaking community in a role analogous to the one exercised elsewhere by the elders. What is important for present purposes is the recognition that fixed patterns of ministry were not laid out from the beginning. As needs arose and as the existing structures were judged inadequate to meet them, new forms developed. Recognized need provoked a creative pastoral response.

Some documents in the New Testament put a greater emphasis on precise forms of ministry than others. Paul, for example, has often been seen as encouraging a more charismatic form of church order than other more "Catholic" New Testament writings. But even in Paul one finds indications that the Christian community was never simply amorphous or purely charismatic, however one defines that term. In the oldest of his letters that we have, 1 Thessalonians, Paul urges believers to "respect those who labor among you, and have charge of you in the Lord and admonish you; esteem them very highly in love because of their work" (1 Thes 5:12–13). Some members of the community clearly have a responsibility of leadership, and because of it and because of their efforts, community members are to respect and collaborate with them. At the end of 1 Corinthians Paul suggests that certain people may have come to exercise such roles because they were the first in a given area to accept the gospel. "Brothers and sisters, you know that members of the household of Stephanas were the first converts in Achaia, and they have devoted themselves to the service of the saints; I urge you to put yourselves at the service of such people, and of everyone who works and toils with them" (1 Cor 16:15–16).

At the same time Paul certainly emphasized the positive contribution that all believers were to make to the building up of the church. In introducing the image of the body of Christ, Paul affirms that "there are varieties of gifts, but the same Spirit; and there are varieties of services, but the same Lord; and there are varieties of activities, but it is the same God who activates all of them in everyone. To each is given the manifestation of the Spirit for the common good" (1 Cor 12:4–7). As in a body, so also in the church all members are to be regarded as precious; all are to be encouraged to make their distinctive contributions to the well-being of the whole. As much as Paul insists, however, on the multiplicity and variety of charisms, he does not hesitate to put some order among them: "And God has appointed in the church first apostles, second prophets, third teachers; then deeds of power, then gifts of healing, forms of assistance, forms of leadership, various kinds of tongues" (1 Cor 12:28). The authoritative word of apostles and prophets comes in the first two places and then the interpretative word of the teacher. The church is rooted in and depends to a very great extent for its growth on the gospel, the word of God. Other gifts, including those of leadership, have their own distinctive contribution to make to community life.

What Paul refers to here as leadership and in 1 Thessalonians as "those who labor among you," may well be the same types of people to whom he refers in the address of his letter to the Philippians as *episcopoi* and *diakonoi. Episcopus* means literally "overseer"; it is the Greek equivalent of "bishop." The *diakonoi* are servants, perhaps already what came to be called deacons.

Another key term for the development of Catholic office is *presbyteros,* meaning "elder." Although it is the root word behind "priest," *presbyteros* does not have the same kind of religious overtones as the English word. In the time of Jesus presbyters or elders were not priests but rather lay men who exercised a certain authority in local synagogues. Jewish priests performed their priestly service in the Temple of Jerusalem. Synagogues, on the other hand, were meeting places that could be found throughout the Jewish world and that served as social and religious centers for local communities. It was in the synagogues that Jews gathered on the sabbath for prayers and for the reading of the scriptures. A group of elders was often entrusted with the care and upkeep of the synagogue and with overseeing its functioning.

Jewish Christians seem to have taken over the traditional terminology of presbyter-elder to describe those who exercised roles of responsibility and leadership in their own communities. In the unfolding of the story of the Jerusalem church in Acts, at a certain point a group of elders is shown, in collaboration with James, to be exercising leadership in the community. 1 Peter reflects an analogous situation. Peter writes: "As an elder myself and a witness of the sufferings of Christ, as well as one who shares in the glory to be revealed, I exhort the elders among you to tend the flock of God that is in your charge, exercising the oversight, not under compulsion but willingly, as God would have you do it—not for sordid gain but eagerly. Do not lord it over those in your charge, but be examples to the flock" (1 Pt 5:1–3).

When people are sick, the letter of James instructs believers, "they should call for the elders of the church and have them pray over them, anointing them with oil in the name of the Lord" (Jas 5:14). The pastoral letters talk a good deal about elders and especially about their general moral qualifications One of their chief responsibilities is teaching: "Let the elders who rule well be considered worthy of double honor, especially those who labor in preaching and teaching" (1 Tm 5:17).

The question of church office or of the ordained ministry in the New Testament period is a complicated and controverted one. An adequate handling of it would require far more space than is available in the present context. What is important to note here is that the beginnings of such an office existed in one form or another from the outset and that in the course of the first century the office slowly developed and took on the classical forms and language that have been a part of the Catholic tradition ever since. Initially it seems that leadership in the local churches was exercised by a group, whether they were called presbyters or bishop-overseers. With time one person tended increasingly to play the dominant role and came to be known as the bishop while the rest of the leadership collective formed a council of elders that surrounded him in liturgical gatherings and supported him in his activities. Deacons seem to have been there from a very early date and were actively involved with various community and social needs. As the liturgy became more complex, they took on more important roles in it.

If there are indications in the pastoral letters of a threefold structure of bishop, presbyters, and deacons in local communities, this Catholic model only really emerges clearly with Ignatius of Antioch, a bishop and martyr, who on his way to Rome and under arrest around 115 wrote a series of letters to churches and church leaders in Asia Minor. In the letters it becomes evident that at Antioch and in Asia Minor the classical Catholic pattern has already taken root. It is highly likely that the same pattern was more or less universally adopted throughout the church by the middle of the second century.

We referred briefly in chapter 3 to the growing significance that bishops assumed in the course of the second century and especially in the context of the struggle with heresy. Bishops were regarded as exercising a unique teaching role in the church, due to the double fact that they had been ordained in the succession of the apostles and that through ordination they had received a special charism of truth. We also noted how with time bishops began to meet in local synods to deal with common challenges and concerns; a new level in episcopal collaboration was reached with the calling of the first ecumenical council by Constantine at Nicaea in 325.

In the fourth and fifth centuries there were a remarkable number of bishop theologians who put their stamp not only on their own local communities but on the whole era. The period is regarded by many as a golden age of Catholic Christianity. At the time there still tended to be a bishop in each moderately sized town or city. He presided over the liturgical and pastoral life of the community and was assisted in his duties by a number of presbyters and deacons. Beginning at the end of the second century bishops were sometimes called priests. The background here seems to have been the role they played in the eucharist and in other liturgical celebrations. Just as bishops shared in the pastoral and teaching offices of Christ, so also did they share in his priesthood. As churches grew and as several parishes came to exist in what would come to be called dioceses, presbyters took over in local communities many of the pastoral and liturgical functions of the bishops. As they did, they too began to be referred to as priests.

MEDIEVAL DEVELOPMENTS

Although it is easy to recognize that many medieval forms and practices were rooted in and continued things that were already there in the patristic period, it is no exaggeration to say that modern Roman Catholicism owes a good deal of its distinctiveness to developments that took place during the Middle Ages. This is certainly true of the papacy. From the beginning, the Roman church had a sense of its special character, given that both Peter and Paul had helped to plant the faith in it by their preaching and their martyrdom. With time, this grew into a conviction that Peter in particular remained present and active in a special way in the Roman church and in its bishops. The influence of Rome was heightened by the fact that it was the only one of the five great patriarchal sees of antiquity that existed in the western part of the empire. The subsequent, gradual drifting apart of East and West and the political and social role that the bishops of Rome came to play with the demise of the empire in the West meant that they assumed responsibilities and made claims that were quite different from anything that developed in the East.

The history of the papacy and of its impact on all aspects of Western European life and culture is far too rich and many sided to be even touched on here. What is important to note is that in its struggles to obtain and maintain the liberty of the church vis-à-vis medieval kings and emperors, the role of the papacy within the church itself became much more dominant. A key turning point here was the so-called Gregorian reform of the eleventh century and especially the efforts of Gregory VII (1073–85). The power and the prestige of the papacy experienced periods of both growth and decline. Individual popes varied considerably in ability and in religious commitment. Many were saintly; others lived scandalous lives. In the fourteenth and fifteenth centuries the papacy's moral and spiritual authority was undermined by a period of some seventy years (1305–78) when popes did not even reside at Rome but rather at Avignon in southern France and, immediately following this, by a period of almost thirty years (1378–1417) when there were two popes and briefly at the end three. The Great Schism as it was called was only overcome by the intervention of a council, a fact that contributed to the development of *conciliarism,* a view of the church that emphasized the role of councils over the pope, at least in cases of emergency such as the one that the church had recently undergone.

Another significant development in the medieval period for the distinctively Catholic understanding of the ordained ministry has to do with the priesthood. From a theological point of view, the category of priesthood, of *sacerdotium,* became increasingly central. It was related to the sacraments and especially to the sacrifice of the Mass. The priest became a person empowered by ordination to offer Mass and to administer the other sacraments, especially penance. By this time many monks in individual monasteries were being ordained without any pastoral responsibilities, which reinforced the tendency to understand ordination almost exclusively in terms of its relation to the sacramental order. This one-sided emphasis on the category of priesthood and on the offering of the Mass as the heart of priestly responsibilities led to the anomalous situation where many of the great Scholastic theologians doubted that episcopal ordination was a sacrament. It clearly added something to the priesthood, but this was thought of in terms of jurisdiction and of legal responsibility and empowerment. The result of these developments was an understanding of church office that from a theological perspective was one-sidedly sacramental and narrowly cultic. Whatever preaching and teaching and broader pastoral responsibilities priests had did not seem to flow from their ordination. They were the result of a granting of jurisdiction from a bishop or religious superior. These emphases led to the phenomenon of the Mass-saying priest, the priest who, for whatever reason, failed to exercise any serious preaching and teaching responsibilities.

Another element in the theology of priesthood that developed in this period was the notion of an indelible character. Ordination, like baptism and confirmation, cannot be repeated. Once persons are baptized or ordained, they are marked in a spiritual way so that, even if they become apostates or as priests fail to exercise their office, they remain baptized and ordained members of the community. Once a priest, always a priest. Theologically, a priest, even if legally barred from exercising his ministry, can never fully become a lay person again.

FROM THE REFORMATION TO TRENT AND VATICAN I

Beginning with a reaction against abuses of various kinds, the Protestant reformers rapidly came to a rejection of the papacy when it failed to agree with their analysis of what was needed for church renewal. Eventually both Luther and Calvin regarded the pope as the anti-Christ. They also repudiated the episcopacy, at least in the form in which it then existed, because they saw it failing in its responsibilities in regard to the gospel.

As far as the priesthood was concerned, Luther denied its specifically priestly character. He recognized the importance of ordained ministry in the church, but he appealed to the fact that ministry is nowhere described in the New Testament in priestly language. The only priesthood in addition to that of Christ is the priesthood of all the baptized. He also denied that ordination is a sacrament in any technical sense of that term. Christian ministers are not fundamentally different from other believers. They fulfill certain functions or tasks, especially those of preaching and of presiding at the sacraments, but they are not in their very being different from others. Those ministers who cease to exercise their responsibilities and return to the lay state are what they were before ordination—lay persons. There is no such thing as an indelible character that sets off the ordained from the non-ordained.

In responding to Luther, the council of Trent did not attempt to offer what might be called a complete theology of the ordained ministry. It did not, for example, go into the question of the precise relationship between pope and bishops, because this issue continued to be debated among Catholics themselves. Through his legates who presided at the council, the pope instructed the bishops to focus on those aspects of the Catholic tradition Luther had denied. The result was not a balanced overview of the issues but a somewhat one-sided response to the one-sided reaction of Luther and the others to the medieval developments.

Trent insisted on the priestly character of the ministry: "Sacrifice and priesthood are so joined together by God's foundation that each exists in every law." And therefore, as Christ instituted the eucharist as a sacrifice, so must he have made the apostles and their successors priests and entrusted to them the power "to consecrate, offer and administer his body and blood, as also to remit or retain sins" (Trent, session 23, ch. 1). Ordination is a sacrament and it imparts a character that sets the ordained off from lay persons. Although Trent was conscious of the need for a renewal of preaching and called for it in its reform decrees, in its dogmatic treatment of ordination the focus was almost exclusively on sacraments and on the fact that priests are empowered to administer them through ordination.

Brief mention should be made here of Vatican I (1869–70), which defined papal primacy and papal infallibility. In doing so it brought a development in Catholicism that can be traced back to Gregory VII in the eleventh century to a historical and theological climax. In the course of the eight hundred years that separated Gregory from the council, the role of the papacy in the church, whatever its changing fortunes in the world at large, continued to grow. This growth was not always at the same rate, nor was it without real opposition, opposition, for example, from medieval conciliarists and the Protestant reformers and from national church movements in Germany and France and elsewhere in the seventeenth and eighteenth centuries. In spite of such opposition and in part stimulated by it, the claims of popes and the acceptance of those claims by the Catholic community continued until at Vatican I papal centralization or *ultramontanism,* as it was called, was solemnly endorsed by the bishops themselves. Some bishops argued, for a variety of reasons, against the definition of papal infallibility and left before the final vote was taken, but they all eventually assented to it.

Primacy of jurisdiction means that all authority in the church rests ultimately in the hands of the pope. What was actually defined on the point is summarized in the concluding canon:

> If anyone says that the Roman pontiff has merely an office of supervision and guidance, and not the full and supreme power of jurisdiction over the whole church, and this not only in matters of faith and morals, but also in those which concern the discipline and government of the church dispersed throughout the whole world; or that he has only the principal part, but not the absolute fullness, of this supreme power; or that this power of his is not ordinary and immediate both over all churches and each of the churches, and over all and each of the pastors and faithful: let him be anathema. (*First Dogmatic Constitution on the Church of Christ,* chapter 3)

The precise meaning of the text and how best to translate it into structures and practices was not immediately clear. What made it initially more difficult was that the council's teaching on the pope stood by itself and was not related, for example, to the traditional Catholic understanding of the role of bishops and of ecumenical councils. Vatican I had intended to produce a document dealing with the whole of ecclesiology, and a draft had been prepared for its deliberation, but the threat of a war between France and Germany led to the adjourning of the council without any discussion of it. The withdrawal of French soldiers from Rome allowed the troops of the *risorgimento,* the movement for Italian unification, to take the city on September 20, 1870. This resulted in the dissolution of the Papal States and brought to an end a thousand year period in papal history. It also put the pope into an anomalous situation as he became more or less a prisoner in the Vatican palace in the midst of the new Italian state. It was only in 1929 that the pope's position was normalized when the Lateran Accords were signed with the Italian government thus creating the situation that still exists today—an independent Vatican City in the middle of Rome.

The combination of the definitions of Vatican I and the plight of the papacy between 1870 and 1929 contributed to a heightened awareness in the Catholic world of the pope and of his role in the church. Catholicism was probably never more unified or centralized than it was in the period from Vatican I to Vatican II.

VATICAN II AND COLLEGIALITY

John XXIII surprised a great many people in the Catholic Church when on January 25, 1959, he announced his intention to convoke an ecumenical council. Because of the teaching of Vatican I on papal primacy and infallibility, some theologians had come to believe that there would never be another council. If the pope has the fullness of power in the church and if in his teaching office he is capable of coming to infallible judgments, then what purpose could a council possibly serve? The calling of the council brought back to the consciousness of Catholics the importance of the conciliar tradition and the considerable contribution that great councils in the past had made to the life of the church.

In outlining his hopes for Vatican II, Pope John remained at a fairly general level. He spoke of the renewal of Christian life

and of an *aggiornamento,* an updating, of structures and language. He made clear his desire that the council not be condem-
natory but rather positive in its approach to the contemporary
world. He also wanted the council to serve the cause of Christian
unity. He asked explicitly that it deal with Catholic-Jewish relationships and make an effort to overcome past failings of the
church in this area.

It was during the first session of the council in the fall of
1962 that a more specific agenda was worked out by the bishops
themselves and especially by conciliar leaders such as Cardinal
Suenens of Belgium and Cardinal Montini of Milan. They
believed that the council should focus on the theme of the
church and deal with both its inner life and its relationship with
other religious communities and with the modern world. In
regard to the hierarchical nature of the church, an effort was to
be made to complement the work of Vatican I. This meant, above
all, trying to define the role of the bishops and the relationship
between them and the pope. Here the very experience of the
council became an inspiration and a topic of reflection. The key
category in which the debate was carried out was *collegiality.* The
basic insight here was that bishops are not to be considered simply as individuals responsible for their individual dioceses. To
become a bishop is to become a member of the order or college
of bishops of which the pope is both member and head. An
appeal was made to the fact that Peter himself was both the
leader and a member of the original twelve. If the pope is the
successor of Peter, then all the bishops together are successors of
the original apostolic group. Together with the pope the college
of bishops has a responsibility for the universal church and with
and under the pope has the fullness of authority for its direction.

Vatican II in no sense denied or undermined the teaching
of Vatican I on the papal office. Rather it tried to place what it
said in a new context by adding something about the role of bishops. Common sense indicates that a universal church can benefit
from an active participation in its leadership by people from
around the world. This was part of the experience of the council
itself. Bishops learned from one another and from groups of
bishops representing other parts of the church. Their efforts to

renew church teaching in so many areas from liturgy to ecumenism, the importance of religious freedom, and the need for dialogue with people of other religions, represented for everyone at the council a whole new experience of church leadership. Together with the pope the bishops lived collegiality and exercised it on a scale that was new in church history.

One of the great desires of Paul VI at the end of the council was to find some appropriate manner in which the conciliar experience could be continued. To this end he established the synod of bishops, a regular meeting of representatives of the world episcopate that since 1967 has met more or less every three years and has dealt with a range of topics including justice, the priesthood, family life, catechetics, evangelization, the laity, and religious life. Over the years a number of bishops have regretted that the synods have no decision-making power and are regarded as simply consultative to the pope. Some have also complained that the way they are organized precludes as open and honest an exchange of ideas as they believe is necessary. In spite of such difficulties, the synod represents something new in the history of modern Catholicism, something that balances to some degree the one-sided emphasis on the papacy that marked the pre-conciliar period.

Concern for collegiality has also had an influence on the increased emphasis that has been given since the council to national conferences of bishops. In the modern period there was a tendency for Rome to relate directly to individual bishops. The challenge of implementing the council's many recommendations and decisions, however, required collaborative action on the part of bishops in different countries and regions and language groupings. In the period immediately following Vatican II, North American bishops responded enthusiastically to this challenge and in the process created new bonds among themselves. More recently the precise role of such conferences has become a focus of a debate, the nature of which will be touched on in chapter 6. For now it is enough to note that the fact of national conferences and the considerable role they have played since the council reflect a genuine desire on the part of the Catholic Church to find a balance between the papal and the episcopal poles in its understanding of church structures. That such a balance is not easy to establish is manifest from the conflicts and tensions that have marked the post-conciliar period. That balance must continue to be sought, both for the good of the Catholic Church and for the cause of Christian ecumenism, should be obvious.

THE ORDAINED MINISTRY AND THE THREEFOLD OFFICE OF CHRIST

If the unifying theological theme running through most of the documents of Vatican II is the church, a secondary theme that surfaces again and again and that acts finally as a key to much of the council's ecclesiology is that of the threefold office of Christ. Jesus is identified as priest, prophet, and king. (The second term is sometimes replaced by "teacher" and the third by "shepherd.") The original three go back to the early church and are related to the basic title, Messiah or Christ. The Christ is the anointed one, and in Israel's history priests, prophets, and kings were all either actually anointed with oil or thought of, as in the case of the great prophets, as anointed with the Spirit. Calvin was the first theologian to make the three offices the starting point for his presentation on Christ's saving activity. In the course of the nineteenth century the same pattern was applied by Catholic theologians to the church and especially to church leadership.

In its presentation of the ordained ministry Vatican II does not begin with the priesthood, as medieval theology did, but rather with the episcopate. In this it follows the practice of the patristic church. Bishops are the key to the meaning of church office. Other ordained ministers are to be seen in relation to them. In order to suggest the range of bishops' responsibilities, the council says that they share in the threefold office of Christ, that is, in his priestly, teaching, and pastoral or shepherding functions. In the sacramental structure of the church the bishop in his diocese represents in a special way Christ himself. Through the bishop Christ remains present in the community of faith exercising his priestly, teaching, and shepherding activities. Obviously bishops are sinful and limited human beings like the rest of humanity, but by ordination they are configured sacramentally to

Christ so that in and through their ministerial activity Christ might continue to be present to his church.

What is true of bishops is also true at a secondary level of those who in the tradition are known as presbyters or priests. Although English versions of the conciliar texts have tended to translate both *presbyterus* and *sacerdos* as "priest," the authors of some of the documents at least tried to introduce certain distinctions. To call presbyters priests is to open the way to two possible misunderstandings. It could lead people to disregard the fact that *all* the baptized share in the priesthood of Christ, and it could give the impression that priests have *only* priestly functions and not prophetic and pastoral ones as well. Here Vatican II tried to root everything involved in episcopal and presbyteral ministry in ordination. By being ordained, bishops and presbyters are configured in their distinctive ways with Christ—priest, prophet, and shepherd. They are icons of Christ precisely in his threefold office, not merely in one or another part of it.

As it did in the case of bishops, Vatican II emphasized the collegial nature of the presbyteral office. In being ordained a presbyter, a person becomes part of the order of presbyters and more specifically part of the local presbyterate, which with and under the bishop is responsible for the spiritual well-being of the diocesan church. Both episcopal and presbyteral ministries are profoundly pastoral in orientation. They involve community leadership, which given the nature of the Christian community necessarily entails forms of preaching and teaching as well as presiding at liturgical celebrations. As much as presbyters have a direct relationship through ordination with Christ, they are to exercise their ministry within the community of the church and in a collaborative way with other ministers and with the bishop.

As part of its return to early church practices and convictions, the bishops at Vatican II called for the reestablishment of the permanent diaconate. Deacons played an important role in the first thousand years of church history. Although their precise responsibilities changed in the course of that period, they were for a good part of it a fixed and important element in the ordained ministry. Later the diaconate became nothing more than a steppingstone for young men proceeding to the priesthood.

In recommending the reestablishment of the permanent diaconate the council also expressed the hope that it would be open to mature married men. This represented a dramatic shift in regard to traditional attitudes toward celibacy and made it possible that married people in relatively large numbers would become part of the hierarchical structure of the church. The implementation of the council's recommendations was left to national conferences and to individual bishops. The practice since Vatican II has varied from country to country and from diocese to diocese, but in many places married deacons who continue to work in secular professions and jobs have become a significant part of contemporary Catholic experience and in the process have modified traditional understandings of what is compatible with the ordained ministry.

MINISTRY WITHIN THE COMMUNITY OF FAITH

A number of commentators have pointed to the fact that the treatment of the hierarchy in the council's *Dogmatic Constitution on the Church* occurs only in chapter 3. Chapter 1 is entitled "The Mystery of the Church" and deals primarily with its trinitarian and christological roots and depths. Chapter 2, "The People of God," develops an ecclesiology that puts the emphasis on what all members of the church share in virtue of their baptism. The development focuses on the priestly and prophetic offices in which all the baptized participate. The treatment of the hierarchy comes after this initial overview, which has suggested to many that the bishops wanted to emphasize that church structure or the ordained ministry does not exist outside or above the church but rather within it. Vatican II made the language of ministry its own. Pope, bishops, priests, and deacons, as rooted as they are in the sacramental nature of the church and as important as their contributions are for its well-being, do not exist for themselves. To be ordained in the Catholic Church is to accept a ministry, a service to Christ and the gospel but also to the community of faith. Ministry exists in and for the church. It is meant to help it become ever more authentically God's people, the body of Christ, and the temple of the Spirit, and in doing so to fulfill the mission entrusted to it by Christ.

Because of the intimate relationship between the ordained ministry and the life of the whole community, changes in that life have repercussions on the way the ministry is understood and exercised. In this sense the efforts at Vatican II and since to involve all the faithful in various ways in the life and mission of the church present challenges and offer new possibilities for all levels of the hierarchy. Here we need to recall all that was said in chapter 1 about the council's insistence on such things as the implications of baptism, the importance of the priesthood of the faithful, and the fact of charisms. These and similar emphases break down an older image of the church divided into active and passive elements. Whereas earlier, the clergy sometimes was identified with the active element and the laity with the passive, the ideal of Vatican II is that both are active, although exercising different roles and fulfilling different responsibilities.

One of the more striking developments in the North American church in the post-conciliar period has been the dramatic growth in lay ministry. Lay women and men have become increasingly involved in the life of the church, whether as volunteers or as paid professionals, whether part-time or full-time. Many of them have received a theological education and are recognized in formal ways by diocesan authorities as exercising official ministries. The existence of such people represents an enormous asset but it also presents a challenge to those in positions of authority to integrate them in a positive and helpful way into church structures. At the very least it demands a more collaborative style of leadership than was customary in the past.

At Vatican II the debate about collegiality focused almost exclusively on the bishops and on their relationship with one another and with the pope. Since the council the term has been applied to relationships at every level of church life. It is used to describe the way priests are to relate among themselves and with their bishop as well as the way bishops and priests should relate to the broader community and especially to those lay people who are actively involved in forms of ministry. Common sense already demands that people working together for a common purpose should respect one another and collaborate in every possible way. This becomes all the more imperative if one takes seriously what is implied by baptism and by faith in the presence of the Spirit in the hearts of all believers.

DEBATES ABOUT THE PRIESTHOOD

One of the major surprises of the post-conciliar period was the crisis that the ministerial priesthood underwent. The period began with a great deal of enthusiasm about Vatican II and the renewal process for which it called. The positive response by lay people to the new possibilities that were opening up for them was remarkable. The same could be said about the development in some dioceses of the permanent diaconate. Religious sisters, for their part, were often in the forefront of change. In spite of much that was positive in the reaction of priests, it was not long before many began withdrawing from the active ministry. At the same time the number of those entering seminaries and religious life fell dramatically. The result over the long term has been an obvious aging of the clergy and a decline in numbers.

An issue that was not discussed at the council but which rapidly became a focus of debate after it was celibacy. Since the Middle Ages celibacy has been mandatory for those in major orders in the Western church, whether religious or diocesan. Although it is only a church law, popes and spiritual writers have argued that a special affinity exists between celibacy and priesthood. It has certainly been a distinguishing feature of Catholicism. In the past there have been exceptions, whether of whole churches united to Rome like the Ukrainian Catholic Church or on a more individual basis, as in the recent cases of Anglican and Episcopalian priests becoming Catholic priests.

Pope John Paul II has insisted on the continuing validity of the present discipline and has reiterated forcefully the traditional arguments for its appropriateness. Other church people, including some bishops, have raised the question of whether in a changed world it would not be pastorally wiser to ordain married as well as single people and perhaps, in a way analogous to the Orthodox practice, to foster celibacy primarily within the religious life. However this debate will be resolved, celibacy embraced for the sake of the kingdom will continue in some form or another to be a value that Catholicism will foster and try to live.

More controversial and more difficult has been the issue of the ordination of women. This was not even mentioned at the council but in the late 1960s and 1970s became a focus of discussion and conflict. Reference was made in chapter 2 to the 1976 document of the Congregation for the Doctrine of the Faith on the topic. John Paul II has reiterated its teaching on a number of occasions and in an apostolic letter in 1994 reinforced it with all of his authority. For him the issue is not disciplinary but rather touches on questions of faith. It is therefore something that the church is unable to change. "Wherefore, in order that all doubt may be removed regarding a matter of great importance, a matter which pertains to the church's divine constitution itself, in virtue of my ministry of confirming the brethren (cf. Lk 22:32) I declare that the church has no authority whatsoever to confer priestly ordination on women and that this judgment is to be definitively held by all the church's faithful" (*Ordinatio sacerdotalis,* no. 4).

In spite of this solemn declaration by the pope, many Catholics including theologians have continued to argue that the question needs to be discussed further. A major concern is that the non-ordination of women could be interpreted as reflecting a negative view of women and of their capacity for religious leadership. The debate, as already suggested, touches on many issues that are fundamental to Catholic identity, including authority, tradition, and development.

However the present debates about the ministerial priesthood are resolved, it is clear that the ordained ministry is at the heart of Catholic life. The concrete forms in which it has existed and the attitudes that have often accompanied it are to a large degree historically conditioned. There is much here that is not of the essence of the office and that could be changed. That there is such an office in the church, however, and that it is more than a merely functional role that any baptized person can fulfill is part of what is most distinctive of the Catholic experience of Christianity. God's gifts to the church include not only word and sacrament but also the ordained ministry, a key responsibility of which is to proclaim the word and to preside at sacramental celebrations. Both of these are part of a broader responsibility to exercise pastoral leadership.

MINISTRY AND COMMUNION

Catholic Christianity has always given a certain priority to structure and organization. It may well have been influenced in this by the administrative and legal genius that it inherited from the Roman Empire. Over the centuries its involvement in various ways in the political and other structures of Western society forced it to formulate and defend its freedom and its rights against them. The struggle of popes in particular to maintain the independence of the church and of church offices in the face of royal and imperial encroachment deepened the Catholic appreciation of strong structures and legal safeguards. The efforts of the church to defend its institutional rights against twentieth-century dictators echoed and continued in a different world practices and attitudes that date back to the Middle Ages.

Deeper even than this preoccupation with rights and powers has been the Catholic conviction about the sacramental nature of the ordained ministry. The growth of church leadership in the course of the first century was not simply a response to sociological or other factors. Although such things obviously played a part, in the eyes of faith it was the Spirit-inspired community recognizing and developing the structures that would on the one hand ensure its continuing connection to its apostolic origins and on the other would allow it to fulfill its mission in the world. Although much about its concrete forms bear the mark of history, the ordained ministry in what is most central to it transcends all historical conditioning. It belongs to the essence of the church.

The great insight of Vatican II was that church office has to be understood within the community of faith. If in the period leading up to the council there was a tendency to think of the church as a pyramid with the pope at the top, and the laity at the bottom, and bishops and priests in between, the image that corresponds with the conciliar vision is more that of a circle within which everyone is called to play a positive role but within which also there is a given structure, an organization, that is meant to serve and build up the life of the whole. Part of the way that it does this is by stimulating and coordinating the contributions of individual members.

The church is primarily a religious reality, a communion of life. At the deepest level it is a sharing in the mysterious life of the triune God, a communion with the Father in Christ and through the power of the Spirit. The communion of life with God is inseparable from communion with other believers and in some sense with all of God's children. Within the church—that organized and structured community that recognizes and celebrates Christ and his gifts and tries to live out of them—the ordained ministry is a key element. It provides at different levels a focus of unity and forms of leadership. It has a particular responsibility for handing on and preaching the gospel message and for gathering local communities together for the celebration of the sacraments. At the present time it has a special responsibility to encourage individual believers to develop their gifts and talents and to put them at the service of the church and of the world.

For most Catholics this communion is experienced at the level of the local parish. The form of the ordained ministry that most immediately encounters them is that of the parish priest. Local communities, however, experience a broader unity at the diocesan level. Here the bishop is the focal point of unity and shared ministry and mission. National and regional churches are served in analogous ways by national and international conferences of bishops. On the universal level the center of Catholic unity is the pope, the bishop of Rome. As the heir of the ministry of Peter, he has to exercise a concern for all the churches. Through him national churches become aware of one another and of the universal church. For the church to be what Christ intended it to be, collaboration and collegiality at all levels are essential. All ministry in the church, whether lay or ordained, is meant to be a service of God and Christ and of the community. Ultimately rooted in the diakonia, the self-giving love of Jesus, those who exercise it are called to reflect his attitudes in their life and work.

CHAPTER SIX

Unity and Diversity

There is a tension, almost a paradox, implied in the expression *Roman Catholicism.* The second word in the phrase suggests universality. To have a catholic taste in music is to be open to and to have an appreciation for a wide range of musical forms and styles, from the classical to the popular, from chamber music to symphonies, from opera to jazz and Broadway musicals. Using the term in more or less the same general sense, a catholic religion would be one that embraces all genuine values and is at home in all parts of the globe.

A claim to universality should presuppose an openness to pluralism and diversity. One of the most striking things about human beings is how different they are from one another, different as individuals but different also in terms of the various national and regional groupings to which they belong. One of the glories of human creativity is the rich array of languages and cultures that humans have produced. Nor are such things to be thought of in any sense as only surface experiences. The great religions of the world reflect profound but diverse intuitions into life and its meaning. Any attempt to water down human differences in the service of a one-sidedly scientific and technological culture or as a means to facilitate the further expansion of Western consumerism would be rejected by most reflective people as destructively antihuman.

By describing itself as catholic, the church is at least implicitly making claims about its capacity to live with and appreciate pluralism and to enter into a positive relationship with as many different cultures and situations as possible. The word *Roman,* on the other hand, points to a single city and its church, and to the particular language, culture, and tradition that they embody. The very particularity of the reference suggests that the Roman church acts in some way as a norm and criterion for Catholicism, that it is at the very least a focus of Catholic unity.

How one relates these two words and the respective values they evoke has a considerable impact on the way one thinks about Catholicism and about what it should be emphasizing and trying to reflect in its life. In the period leading up to Vatican II, Catholic preoccupation was much more with unity than with diversity. At certain times and in particular areas of church life unity became all but interchangeable with uniformity. This was something in which, on a popular level, many Catholics took considerable pride.

ONE LITURGY, ONE LANGUAGE

One of the most obvious and distinctive features of the preconciliar church and one that struck both Catholics and non-Catholics alike was that the same liturgy was celebrated in the same language throughout much of the Catholic world. The sense of uniformity was heightened by the fact that most Latin-rite Catholics had little or no awareness of the distinctive patterns of Eastern-rite Catholics. They knew simply that whether in New York or Manilla, Berlin or Mexico City, the Mass was celebrated in more or less the same way and above all in the same language. Latin was an extraordinary bond of unity among people who came from very different linguistic backgrounds. Even those who knew little or no Latin knew that it was the language of the liturgy and that as such it united them with worshipers on every continent and in every region of the globe.

Although Latin was the language of the ancient Romans, the first Christians in the capital of the empire were largely Greek-speaking and celebrated the liturgy in their own tongue. Greek was also the language of the New Testament and for that reason was cherished along with Hebrew as having a sacred character. Gradually the Roman church embraced more Latin-speaking members, and as it did it began to carry out its liturgical rituals in that language as well. Latin, in other words, became common in the liturgy of the church at Rome precisely when it did because by that time it had become the vernacular of the majority of its members. Latin remained the dominant language of Western European culture for several centuries, even after the Romance languages had begun to develop and Western Christendom had come to include Germanic and other northern peoples. Throughout the medieval period Latin was the language of the church and of culture, education, and international relations. Because of its role in the liturgy, it took on a special aura and became the third of the sacred languages. The exclusive use of Latin combined with other factors to make the liturgy increasingly something that belonged in a special way to the clergy and which they performed for the laity.

The issue of language in regard to both the Bible and the liturgy was very much at the fore at the time of the Protestant Reformation. The development of the printing press reinforced a tendency that was already present in the fifteenth century to produce vernacular translations of the Bible and to make them available to the people. Luther took the process to a new level. His vernacular version of the New Testament and then of the whole Bible represents a historic moment in the development of the German language. The vernacular Bible and a number of theological tracts also written in German were key instruments in the spread of reformation ideas. Luther's insistence on the normativity of the scriptures and on the centrality of faith to Christian life made him reject the use of Latin in the liturgy. Both word and sacrament proclaim God's gift to us in Christ and in doing so call forth a response of faith in the hearts of the gathered community. For this to happen people need to understand what is being proclaimed in the celebrations. All the reformers followed Luther in his demand that the liturgy be in the vernacular.

Although the German emperor and many Catholic bishops petitioned the pope and the council of Trent to allow the use of the vernacular in the liturgy, the decision was taken to maintain the traditional practice. The one concession to Luther's concerns that Trent was willing to make was a directive given to priests to instruct the faithful during the Mass about its various parts and their meaning. The reason for insisting on Latin is not spelled out in the conciliar documents, but it clearly had to do partly with the traditional practice and partly with the fear that an approval of the vernacular could be misinterpreted as indicating at least partial agreement with some of the doctrinal views of the reformers. In the face of the enormous losses that the Reformation represented for the Catholic Church, Trent opted to strengthen the identity and sense of unity of those who remained loyal to Rome. Its doctrinal statements offered Catholics a clear and precise definition of traditional faith over against what were perceived as the novelties of the reformers. The insistence on Latin and the call for a renewed and uniform text for the Mass were also meant to serve the cause of unity. The new Roman Missal, published in 1570, represents a decisive turning point in the history of the liturgy. The weight it gives to the precise words and gestures that every priest has to follow under pain of sin in celebrating Mass inaugurated a period characterized by *rubricism,* an excessive preoccupation with the minutiae of liturgical norms. With minor changes the liturgy of the Mass as spelled out in the Missal of Pius V remained in force until the renewal brought about by Vatican II.

UNITY OF AUTHORITY, THEOLOGY, AND LAW

If the liturgy was the most visible expression of and means for fostering Catholic unity in the modern period, it was in no sense the only one. As the nineteenth century progressed the Catholic Church felt itself increasingly at odds with many of the dominant trends in Western culture. The French Revolution, in spite of the efforts at restoration that followed the Congress of Vienna (1815), brought about a profound shift in European political and social life. The monarchy and the social arrangements that were a part of the ancien régime were in decline. The future belonged to the middle class and to democracy, to science and technology, and to a more secular world order. The Christian churches to some degree and the Catholic Church to a considerable degree found themselves increasingly at odds with major aspects of contemporary developments. The opposition between the Catholic Church and the new ideas came to a head in the progressive loss of the Papal States in the 1860s to the forces of the Italian *risorgimento.*

When Pius IX became pope in 1845, there was a perception in many parts of Europe that in some areas at least he might be sympathetic to liberal concerns. After the revolutionary upheavals of 1848 drove him from Rome, however, he took a much more negative view of contemporary trends. The famous 1864 *Syllabus of Errors* seemed to set the pope and the Catholic Church as a whole against much that was cherished by contemporary liberal theorists: freedom of the press, freedom of religion, the separation of church and state, and divorce, as well as the more typical ideologies of the age including rationalism and materialism. Because the document was made up of a series of eighty quotations from earlier writings of the pope and because each of them was formulated negatively, the precise import of what was being said was difficult to judge. Symbolically, however, the syllabus was widely understood to represent a fundamentally negative response by the pope to much of what was distinctive about the new world that was coming to birth in European society.

We have seen that the most dramatic and far-reaching achievement of Vatican I was its definition of papal primacy and infallibility. At the very time that the pope was losing the age-old basis for his political power and independence—the papal states—his position in the church was becoming stronger than ever before. The combination of the forceful and winning personality of Pius IX, the doctrinal definitions of Vatican I, and the unresolved conflict between the pope and the new Italian state, made Catholics in the last decades of the nineteenth century more conscious of and identified with the pope than at any earlier period. The failure of Vatican I to produce its intended document on the church, which at the very least would have provided a context for understanding its statement on the papacy, reinforced this tendency. For many Catholics the church and the pope had become all but identical.

The outstanding quality of Pius IX's successors together with the enormous upheavals that European society underwent in the course of the first half of the twentieth century continued and deepened the special affection and respect with which Catholics surrounded the pope. It was at the beginning and end of this period that the only examples of a pope solemnly defining a dogma of the church are to be found. Pius IX defined the immaculate conception of Mary as part of Catholic faith in 1850, and Pius XII defined the assumption in 1954.

The pontificate of Pius IX (1845–78) also witnessed the triumph of neo-Scholasticism. The original Scholastics included a number of outstanding philosophers and especially theologians who taught at medieval universities. Neo-Scholasticism was a form of Catholic thought that developed in the mid-nineteenth century and that sought in the great medieval theologians and philosophers an inspiration and a help for responding to the challenges of modern philosophy and to modern attacks in general on the truth of traditional Christianity. Because of the nature of the opposition against which it reacted, the movement tended to be more philosophical than theological. The theology that was developed was formulated in a somewhat abstract, even rationalistic manner. It made relatively little use of the scriptures or of the thought and practice of the early church. With Vatican I, neo-Scholasticism received an initial endorsement. In subsequent decades it became the official philosophy and theology of the Catholic Church and, as such, was a required object of study in seminaries around the world. In spite of the real ability of some of the neo-Scholastics themselves, their thought, as something that was imposed by authority, functioned for many people as a kind of ideology. Catholic priests and teachers, no matter where they lived or in what context they did their teaching, were encouraged to give the same answers and to offer the same explanations. Thus the unity of the liturgy was echoed and reinforced by the unity of content and of method that was so much a part of the teaching that took place in nearly all Catholic institutions between 1870 and 1950.

In 1918 a new code of canon law was promulgated for the Catholic Church. It came out of and gave legal expression to the increased emphasis on unity and centralization that was so characteristic of the post–Vatican I church. The code provided a handy summary of Catholic liturgical and community life in so far as this could be translated into legal norms. Applying almost everywhere throughout the Catholic world, the code represented another significant factor in the fostering of unity and, to some degree, of uniformity.

To recapitulate briefly: the intense preoccupation of Catholicism in the modern period with unity, as much as it was motivated by positive Catholic values, served to strengthen the church in the face of opposition. This was clearly the case at the time of Trent and of the Protestant Reformation, but it was also the case in the nineteenth and early twentieth centuries. The opposition now was the Enlightenment and the new social and political order that had resulted from the French and American revolutions. From the seventeenth century onward, in a series of wave-like movements, a new world was developing in Western European society. For lack of a better word, one might call it *modernity*. In many ways the new world grew up in conscious opposition to Christianity and especially to the Catholic Church. The result was that many church people felt themselves threatened by it. In order to respond to modernity, the church returned to its own rich past for inspiration. It emphasized traditional forms of life and traditional ways of doing theology. It also reinforced the role of the pope. A strong papacy became a focal point of Catholic unity and a bulwark against secular society. Attempts by various Catholics in the course of the nineteenth century and again at the turn of the twentieth century to reach out in a more open and collaborative way to the newer trends were regarded as acts of disloyalty and as destructive of Catholic identity and unity.

VATICAN II, AN EXPERIENCE OF CATHOLICITY

It is only when one situates the teaching of Vatican II against the background of the previous two hundred years of church history that one begins to appreciate its significance. The council itself was a profound learning experience, not only for many of the bishops who took part in it but also for Catholics at large who followed its proceedings. In sheer numbers and in the variety of national, ethnic, and linguistic traditions that its members represented, Vatican II was the most universal council of church history. Thanks to the concerted efforts of Pius XII many of the bishops who came from Africa, India, and the Orient were indigenous to the churches they represented. There were still a number of missionary bishops, but the process of indigenization of the hierarchy was well advanced in all parts of the globe.

Some of the most important and long-ranging effects of the council resulted from the simple fact that as it unfolded bishops learned from one another about the variety of challenges and opportunities that confronted Catholics in different parts of the world. North American bishops came with their own experiences and concerns. Although these had a great deal in common with the experiences and concerns of Western European bishops, they were very different from those of bishops from Latin America or Africa or Asia. They were different, too, from those of bishops living in countries dominated by Soviet Russia. The more concrete the discussions at the council became, the more obvious it was that situations around the Catholic world varied enormously. Attitudes toward marriage, problems of justice, interreligious dialogue, ecumenism: such things were not the same everywhere and therefore the effort to say something on such topics had to consider a wide variety of situations and leave room for adaptation at the local level.

The theme of collegiality has implications for catholicity. The insistence on the collegial nature of the episcopacy naturally led to a renewed sense of the importance of groupings of bishops at various levels. If a council as the gathering of all the bishops of the world is a privileged expression of episcopal collegiality, then smaller groups of bishops on national and regional levels are at least partial expressions of the same reality. The multiplicity and variety of the churches represented by the bishops is at the heart of catholicity. The one church is present in the many churches. Everywhere the community of faith gathers around its bishop, Christ is present to his church. The coming together of the bishops at Vatican II implied a coming together in them of all the churches from the Catholic world.

The council was itself an experience of unity in diversity and of diversity in unity. The bishops were strikingly different from one another, different in their backgrounds and education and experiences, but different, too, in terms of the churches and areas of the globe that they represented. The more authentically they spoke out of their own experience, the more they helped to deepen their colleagues' sense of catholicity. At the same time the council was marked by a profound unity. The bishops had come together in Rome in the great basilica dedicated to St. Peter. Everything they did was done in the closest collaboration with the pope. While they were only on ceremonial occasions in St. Peter's, both John XXIII during the first session and Paul VI during the other three were intimately involved with every step of the conciliar process. At its conclusion Paul VI approved and signed with the bishops all the documents that they had passed. The council was a celebration of Catholic unity every bit as much as of Catholic diversity.

ADAPTATION AND PLURALISM

The theme of adaptation arose in the first place in discussions about the liturgy. Although initially much debated, a decision was soon arrived at to allow the use of the vernacular for at least part of the liturgy. In fact, this turned out to be so successful that very early in the post-conciliar period those involved with carrying out the liturgical renewal sought and obtained the approval of the pope for making the whole of the liturgy available in the vernacular. Even the beginnings, however, of the process made clear that everything could not be determined by a single committee working in Rome but would have to involve national hierarchies and bishops from different language groups in order to ensure the adequacy of the translations.

The new liturgy has a great deal more flexibility than the old. In many cases there are choices among various prayers and scripture readings. The priest is encouraged at times to express certain things in his own words. All this indicates a shift away from the preoccupation with uniformity that was so characteristic of the renewal that came out of Trent. Vatican II went further than this in its document on the liturgy in talking about more extensive forms of adaptation, especially for mission countries. The general principle is clear: "Provided that the substantial unity of the Roman rite is preserved, provision shall be made, when revising the liturgical books, for legitimate variations and adaptations to different groups, regions, and peoples, especially in mission countries" (*Constitution on the Sacred Liturgy*, no. 38). A little further on it speaks of cases where "an even more radical adaptation of the liturgy is needed" and lays out the process of experimentation and approval that such adaptations will have to undergo (no. 40).

The Vatican II document that speaks most explicitly about pluralism and its value is, not surprisingly, the document on ecumenism. If there is ever going to be an organic union among the Christian churches, it will not be by all but one of them losing their identity and simply becoming members, for example, of the Roman Catholic Church. Any talk of unity in the context of ecumenism has to be of a unity that admits and indeed rejoices in and fosters diversity.

In a chapter entitled "Principles of Catholic Ecumenism," all Catholics are encouraged "while preserving unity in essentials ...[to] preserve a proper freedom in the various forms of spiritual life and discipline, in the variety of liturgical rites, and even in the theological elaboration of revealed truth." The text goes on to say that if Catholics "are true to this course of action, they will be giving ever richer expression to the authentic catholicity and apostolicity of the church" (*Decree on Ecumenism*, no. 4). In speaking a little later about the differences between the Eastern and Western churches, the document states that "far from being an obstacle to the church's unity, such diversity of customs and observances only adds to her beauty and contributes greatly to carrying out her mission" (no. 16). This applies not only to liturgy and devotional practices but to theological developments as well. The council reveals a remarkable openness to the distinctive theological traditions of the East and says that "these various theological formulations are often to be considered complementary rather than conflicting" (no. 17).

A similar sensitivity to the positive meaning of diversity comes out in *Pastoral Constitution on the Church in the Modern World*, the document on the church in the modern world. The whole document presupposes a dynamic sense of history and of culture. In reflecting on what the church has received from the world and especially "from the progress of the sciences and from the riches hidden in various cultures," it affirms that "the church learned early in its history to express the Christian message in the concepts and language of different peoples and tried to clarify it in the light of the wisdom of their philosophers; it was an attempt to adapt the gospel to the understanding of all.... This kind of adaptation...must ever be the law of all evangelization." What was true of the past is true today with the difference that the rate of cultural change has increased dramatically and that people are increasingly aware of cultural pluralism. The document goes on to refer to ways in which the church, as a visible, social structure, can learn from "the evolution of social life." It can help it understand its Christ-given constitution "more deeply, express it better, and adapt it more successfully to our times" (no. 44).

Although the above references are in no way exhaustive, it should be clear from them, as it was clear to the bishops who were at the council, that Vatican II represents a significant turning point in regard to the Catholic attitude to the issue of unity and diversity. Unity remains basic and is something for which the pope and the bishops have a special responsibility. Catholic unity, however, does not mean uniformity. It is open to and enriched by a plurality of cultures and countries, languages and philosophies. The limits of plurality, of course, could not be spelled out by the council. That diversity must never undermine the fundamental unity of the church is evident, but when a limit in any given case is reached is very difficult to say beforehand.

IMPLEMENTING THE CONCILIAR VISION

As important an achievement as Vatican II was in itself, its real meaning for the life of the church depended and continues to depend upon the way that its decisions and recommendations are understood and given concrete form in local communities around the world. A technical term for this process is *reception*. It is something to which all believers contribute but perhaps especially religious, priests, bishops, and experts of various kinds. What was particularly important initially was the role of national conferences of bishops. That they had a role to play in the implementation of the liturgical renewal as well as in other areas was spelled out in the conciliar documents themselves.

One of the single most influential events in the post-conciliar period in the Western hemisphere was the meeting of Latin American bishops in Medellín, Columbia, in 1968. The overall theme of the conference was the implementation of Vatican II within the context of Latin American society. Although a wide range of topics was discussed, including evangelization, the liturgy, and the renewal of religious life, a particular emphasis was given to the themes of justice and peace. In the course of the twentieth century the Catholic Church has made a sustained effort to develop an understanding of modern economic and political issues in the light of basic human morality and of the gospel. Although the focus of the effort tended initially to be the situation of workers within capitalist societies, John XXIII with *Pacem in terris* (1963) and Paul VI with *Populorum progressio* (1967) expanded it to embrace worldwide issues, especially those confronting the Third World. Paul VI underlined the interdependence of the two themes of justice and peace. In the modern context, justice, he argued, is the new name for peace. Inspired by this tradition and by Vatican II's Pastoral Constitution on the Church in the Modern World, the bishops at Medellín offered an analysis of the political and economic situation in their own countries and made suggestions about changes that needed to be made if justice were ever to be achieved and real social peace to become a reality. The importance given to this debate and the methodology that the bishops embraced in the course of it gave a considerable impulse to the development of what soon came to be widely known as liberation theology.

Although there was no one defining act in the North American experience analogous to Medellín, both American and Canadian conferences of bishops were extremely active in the post-conciliar period. There was a widespread sense among the bishops of both countries that an adequate reception of Vatican II required the development of programs that would help their churches, while remaining in Catholic unity, to become more deeply rooted in their respective cultures. Although the activities of the two conferences touched on all aspects of church life, their most widely known publications addressed broader social, political, and economic issues. American statements on war and peace and on the economy broke new ground not only in what they said but in the way in which they came to be written. Widespread consultations and the publication and criticism of draft documents made the final texts more reflective of the whole American Catholic Church than a purely episcopal publication could have been.

If a major focus of concern in the North American church in recent decades has been social justice, inculturation has been high on the agenda of conferences of bishops in Africa and Asia in the same period. Here the differences between European and local cultures are far more marked than in North America. The need for a process of inculturation in many areas of church life has been deeply felt. Some of the most creative work in this regard has been in the area of the liturgy. People have creatively integrated into Catholic liturgical practices attitudes, gestures, music, and ritual that reflect what is best in Asian and African cultures. The conferences of bishops have played a key role in the process.

With even these few examples it should be obvious that bishops' conferences came into their own in the post-conciliar period as they tried to implement Vatican II's renewed vision of the life and mission of the church within the context of their respective countries. Beyond making concrete decisions in relation to specific areas, the conferences also helped their members to heighten their awareness of the distinctiveness of the national church and of its place within world Catholicism and to deepen their own sense of corporate responsibility for it. If the church is primarily a communion among all the individual churches of the world, it also involves what might be called intermediary groups, groups existing between the diocese and the universal church. These include national, regional, and linguistic groupings. In Latin America and Africa, in the United Sates and Canada, there are issues and challenges facing Catholics with which dioceses on their own would have trouble dealing. Nothing is more normal than that bishops from all the dioceses of a country or region consult and plan and make decisions together about matters confronting all their churches.

The increased activity of episcopal conferences has on occasion brought them into conflict with individual members and congregations of the Roman Curia. Bishops have sought to widen the scope of their decision-making powers. They argue that because they are nearer to the pastoral challenges and opportunities requiring such decisions, they should be in a position to make them. The Curia, on the other hand, has sometimes sought to restrict the authority of conferences for fear that their activity might undermine overall church unity. Beyond the conflicts and the tensions are different judgments not only about specific cases but more generally about the right balance between unity and diversity. Perhaps, too, the need for control is an issue.

THEOLOGICAL PLURALISM

At the first session of the council the bishops rejected almost all of the draft documents that had been prepared for them. They found them too negative and abstract, not sufficiently biblical or ecumenical. Almost overnight, neo-Scholasticism, the theological tradition that had been dominant in the church for a hundred years, all but disappeared. Even Thomas Aquinas, one of the greatest Catholic theologians and an innovator of considerable intellectual daring, lost the privileged position that he had held in modern Catholicism. In the course of the council and especially in the years immediately following it, philosophical and theological perspectives that for so long had been taken for granted gave way to a radical pluralism of methods and views.

The stimulation to develop new approaches in theology came in part from a desire to enter into dialogue with modern and contemporary trends of thought. In many cases it involved a reaction against the negativity with which the church had tended to regard modern philosophy and modern culture in general. Because modernity itself was far from unified, this turn to the modern involved a pluralism of positions. Some theologians were attracted by existential philosophy, others by Anglo-Saxon process thought, others again by linguistic and hermeneutical philosophies. Non-Europeans sought to relate Catholic faith to the traditions of thought indigenous to their own cultural heritages.

The very nature of theology and the wide range of elements that can enter into it have also contributed to the new pluralism. Some theologians are more biblical in their approach, while others use the dogmatic definitions of the church as an organizing principle for what they want to say. In the post-conciliar period theologians began turning to other disciplines besides philosophy to help them develop and structure their thought. Psychology has played an important role here, as has sociology.

One of the most distinctive and influential of recent developments in Catholic thought has been liberation theology. Although begun in Latin America, it has been taken up by theologians in North America and especially throughout the Third World. The emphasis in this theology, as the word *liberation* suggests, is on situations of oppression, poverty, and injustice, situations that call out for God's intervention, God's salvation. In Latin America such theology has grown up in close contact with small groups of believers confronted by quite specific forms of injustice. People try to understand what their faith has to say to them in such contexts. Their interest is in no sense merely theoretical. They are seeking ways to change the situation and to bring about greater justice for everyone involved in it. This kind of concern demands that one begin with—or at least include—as sophisticated an analysis as possible of the actual conditions. Only such an analysis can help people understand the precise causes of the injustice and suggest ways in which it might be overcome. The biblical texts to which liberation theologians primarily appeal are those which proclaim the values of justice, freedom, and human dignity, and which portray God as actively involved in history on the side of the poor and the oppressed.

Liberation theology has been the focus of some controversy. Some people in Latin America have been threatened by its challenge to the status quo, while some in Rome have questioned whether its emphasis on justice involves a reduction of the gospel message to its social implications. People have also wondered whether its use of Marxist sociological analysis has not opened it to being undermined in some way by some of the more destructive and antireligious elements that are a part of Marxism. Although liberation theology remains somewhat controversial, it represents one of the most creative developments in Catholic thought in the post-conciliar period. It is by definition closely tied to the experience and the context of those who practice it. As such it is an excellent example of how the rediscovery of the catholicity of the church has led to pluralism in theology.

Another example of such pluralism, and one that has had more of an impact on the North American church, is feminist theology. A many-sided social and cultural phenomenon, feminism in the last decades has had an influence on almost all aspects of Western culture. Christian and Catholic women open to the questions and perspectives of feminism have raised new and sometimes radical questions for the church. Feminist thought touches all of theology. It offers a perspective on the Bible and on the history of the church as well as on present issues and practices. Like liberation theology, feminist theology is in no sense unitary; it embraces a variety of positions, all of which concern themselves in some way with the meaning of Christian life and thought for and from the point of view of women.

Catholic feminist theology, like liberation theology, has also been a focus of debate. A major conflict between many feminists and church leadership has been the issue of the ordination of women. In spite of a radical impasse on this topic, the impact of feminist theology on the church at large has been significant and gives no indication of declining. The more women become involved in theology and the more they occupy positions of authority and influence in the church, the more their concerns and perspectives will have to be considered. The most basic pluralism in human life is the duality of the sexes. Traditionally Catholic theology and Catholic decision-making have been carried out almost exclusively by males. As women continue to become more involved in giving direction to Catholic life, this will inevitably change.

A NEW MODEL OF UNITY

Prior to Vatican II the only model of Christian unity that most Catholics could imagine was that of a "return" of other Christians to the unity of the Catholic Church. This was particularly true in the case of the churches and communities that had issued from the Protestant Reformation. In regard to the ancient churches of the East, there was always a sense that their situation was different. Catholics recognized that the Eastern bishops stood in the line of apostolic succession and therefore that the sacramental life of their churches was valid. Vatican II introduced a new perspective in affirming the ecclesial nature of other Christian churches and communities as well. Although it taught that the church of Christ "subsists in the Catholic Church which is governed by the successor of Peter and by the bishops in communion with him" (*Dogmatic Constitution on the Church*, no. 8), it recognized that the church as a theological realtiy existed in other communities as well.

The early years of the post-conciliar period witnessed an enthusiastic involvement of Catholics and of the Catholic Church in the ecumenical movement. Official bilateral dialogues were set up with a number of other churches, and Catholic theologians participated in the work of the Faith and Order Commission of the World Council of Churches. If the initial step in the dialogue was overcoming misunderstanding and prejudice, progress soon proceeded to the point where groups officially appointed by their respective churches were producing agreed statements on a range of issues including the very things that at the time of the Protestant Reformation had been causes of division. The more successful the dialogues were, the more people began to think about the kind of unity for which they were working.

In speaking of the relationship between the Christian East and West, Pope Paul VI referred on various occasions to sister churches. He also used the image of the lungs. Just as a person in order to be in good health needs to be able to breathe through both lungs, so also the church in order to fulfill its mission needs to have both its Eastern and Western parts living together in peace and harmony. Unity here has nothing to do with the absorption of one by the other. Whatever precise form "organic unity" might take, it would involve both churches maintaining and developing their own theological, liturgical, and canonical traditions.

Cardinal Willebrands, the longtime chair of the Secretariat for Christian Unity, suggested that the unity being sought in the ecumenical movement is not that of a single monolithic church but rather of a communion of churches. There would be unity, but a unity that would be compatible with considerable diversity. Although the one faith, the one paschal mystery, would be articulated and celebrated in different ways, all sides would recognize that the differences, while real, would no longer be church dividing. What in detail such a unity would entail is difficult to say. The idea remains rather vague, but it does point in a particular direction. Unity does not mean uniformity; it can and indeed should exist with real pluralism. The great concern is that the pluralism not undermine that basic unity in faith without which there can be no Christian church.

UNITY AND DIVERSITY WITHIN THE NEW TESTAMENT

For some, the post-conciliar concern with pluralism, whether in the context of ecumenism, theology, or liturgical inculturation, appears dangerous to, if not incompatible with, Catholic unity. Concern with pluralism does represent something new in relationship to the century or more that preceded Vatican II; in terms of the longer history of the church, however, it is a return to something that has roots in the New Testament and that achieved classical form in the patristic period. Unity in the early church was always understood to be compatible with a considerable amount of diversity.

The New Testament contains four gospels. Although at times people have sought to reduce them to a single sustained narrative, they really do offer four distinct versions of the life, teaching, and destiny of Jesus. Modern scholarship has brought out with increasing clarity some of the different literary features and theologies that distinguish even Matthew, Mark, and Luke, gospels that in so many ways contain significant parallels. That John's gospel is different from the other three and that it has a theological perspective that is very much its own are obvious to even the casual reader. The gospels themselves thus exemplify the Christian paradox of pluralism within unity. All four tell the story of Jesus and proclaim the saving significance of his life, death, and resurrection, but they do it in ways that reflect the traditions and insights of the communities out of which they come, as well as the theologies of their respective authors.

The pluralism of the New Testament does not stop with the gospels. The rest of it as well—the Acts of the Apostles, the book of Revelation, the Pauline and other letters—all bear witness to the extraordinary variety and vitality that were a part of early Christianity and of the many churches and communities that made it up. The theologies associated with such names as John, Paul, and the author of the letter to the Hebrews are both remarkable and remarkably different. All are one in their affirmation of the salvation that becomes available for humankind in Christ, all are similarly one in recognizing the uniqueness of the person of Jesus, but each formulates the one faith in a distinctive way. The New Testament bears witness to the centrality in Christian experience of both unity and diversity. In Ephesians, Paul begs believers "to lead a life worthy of the calling to which you have been called, with all humility and gentleness, with patience, bearing with one another in love, making every effort to maintain the unity of the Spirit in the bond of peace" (Eph 4:1–3). What Paul says to this one community could easily be said to many communities together. What he asks of them is not based on simple moralism. It is rooted in the nature of the church and in the destiny to which all are called in Christ. "There is one body and one Spirit, just as you were called to the one hope of your calling, one Lord, one faith, one baptism, one God and Father of all who is above all and through all and in all" (Eph 4:4–6). Nor does Paul stop with this appeal to unity. He recognizes that Christian unity exists amid diversity. "But each of us was given grace according to the measure of Christ's gift.... The gifts he gave were that some would be apostles, some prophets, some evangelists, some pastors and teachers, to equip the saints for the work of ministry, for building up the body of Christ, until all of us come to the unity of the faith and of the knowledge of the Son of God, to maturity, to the measure of the full stature of Christ" (Eph 4:7, 11–13). In a striking phrase, Paul offers a principle for growth in Christian maturity, growth also in unity: "Speaking the truth in love," all are to contribute to renewing and deepening the life of the community until it grows up "into him who is the head, into Christ" (Eph 4:15). In the New Testament, church unity is rooted in faith and love and in the saving reality of Christ and in the power of Christ's Spirit. This reality is proclaimed and celebrated and lived in a rich variety of formulations and liturgical prayers and styles of community life.

THE MODEL OF THE EARLY CHURCH

For almost the first three centuries of its existence the church was exposed to threats from both within and without. Reference has already been made to the conflicts and divisions occasioned by divergent interpretations of the gospel and of its implications for moral and community life. These threatened to undermine the unity of both the local and the universal church. Persecution, usually sporadic but sometimes systematic, raised questions about the very survival of Christianity. In the face of such threats efforts were made to reinforce church unity and to defend the developing orthodox understanding of faith. Communities and their bishops took a genuine interest in one another and exchanged letters and visits and consulted on issues of importance. The development of the creeds, the establishment of a canon of New Testament writings, and the meeting together of bishops in local synods all furthered the cause of unity. It was, however, a unity that admitted of a great deal of diversity.

In the fourth and fifth centuries, after the church emerged from its illegal status and became larger, wealthier, and more influential, unity was fostered especially through the ecumenical councils and through the role that the five great patriarchal sees played in their respective regions. The distinctive theological and liturgical traditions developed by the churches of Alexandria and Antioch influenced the many churches that existed within each of their spheres of influence. Rome represented another language and another tradition, a language and tradition that came to dominate the Western church. It was less creative theologically than the Eastern churches but more influential because of its unique prestige and because of the special fidelity with which it was perceived to bear witness to the apostolic tradition. Once Constantinople became the capital of the empire, its church also grew in power and influence. Before long, it exercised a role second only to that of Rome.

The patristic period knew both unity and diversity. That the many churches were all part of the one Catholic Church, the church of Christ, was clear to all observers. That it had a pluralism of languages, liturgies, and popular practices was equally obvious. The diversity inevitably led to misunderstanding, tension, and conflict. Bishops excommunicated one another and cut whole churches off from the bond of unity. Maintaining and fostering unity in that context was not easy, nor was it to be taken for granted. For all the difficulties, however, it was a period of enormous vitality and creativity. Its lesson is clear: a pluralism that does not destroy unity can enrich and deepen it.

The gradual drifting apart of East and West meant that medieval Catholicism would be less pluralistic than the patristic church had been. The increasing importance of the role of the pope throughout the period led to a greater emphasis being put on unity, but it was still a unity that admitted a great deal of diversity: in forms of religious life, in theological approaches, in the changing relations between bishops and pope, in the distinctive national churches and church traditions that developed among the various peoples that made up medieval European society.

If Vatican II in its openness to catholicity and therefore to diversity represented something new in relation to the period that immediately preceded it, that new emphasis was rooted in an older tradition and an earlier practice. The post-conciliar stress on national and regional churches and on the role that conferences of bishops are to play in them has a great deal in common with the Catholic experience of the patristic period. What is perhaps distinctive about Vatican II was its dawning awareness that humanity is living on the threshold of a new historical era. Developments in means of travel and communication along with mass movements of peoples have helped to create among many people a greater sense of global unity and of global diversity than at any time in human history. Vatican II, in its membership and in the range of topics that it addressed, represents, as Karl Rahner has put it, the beginning of a world church. Catholicism has been present to at least some degree in most parts of the globe for some time now. The bishops at the council were animated by a hope and desire that the church would be able to be truly at home on every continent and in every region. Catholics in Africa should be able to be as authentically African in their faith experience as European Catholics are European in theirs. A necessary condition for such a development is a recognition of the possibility and the place for pluralism within Catholic unity.

UNITY AND PLURALISM

Unity embodies a fundamental human and religious value. It is a value that has always been cherished in Catholic Christianity. At the deepest level it is rooted in faith, faith in the oneness of God and in the unity of the divine plan of salvation. There is, as Paul and others put it, one Christ, one Spirit, one baptism. All the baptized are united with Christ and endowed with his Spirit and at the same time are brought into the unity of the church. As the body of Christ, the church cannot but be concerned with unity. A body divided against itself is sick and vulnerable to further division. An organization or society without unity of vision and commitment is unable to achieve the purpose for which it exists.

Much that is central to Catholic Christianity serves the cause of unity. This is true in a very basic way of the canon of scriptures, the creeds, and the whole of the liturgical and sacramental system. These are things Catholics everywhere recognize as essential to their faith and religious life. The apostolic ministry has a special role to play in regard to unity, primarily by safeguarding and handing on the content of the scriptures and the creeds as they have been understood in the Catholic tradition and by overseeing the authenticity of the community's liturgical life. If the individual pastor is meant to be a focus of unity and collaboration in the parish, bishops exercise an analogous responsibility on the diocesan level. Given the range of attitudes and opinions as well as linguistic and ethnic background in many large contemporary dioceses, this episcopal task is by no means an easy one. It requires considerable sensitivity and tact and a genuine love and respect for the various people and groups that make up the diocese.

Bishops working together at the national and regional levels also exercise a real ministry to church unity. People today identify less and less simply with their own diocese; nor do the problems they face as believers exist only at that level. The increased awareness in the post-conciliar period of the national church and of the need for collaborative activity by bishops and others at the national level is a timely and normal development of elements that have been very much a part of the Catholic tradition.

Vatican II and the synod of bishops that was established in its wake have brought back to Catholic awareness something of the great conciliar tradition of Christianity. The college of bishops is meant to serve and build up the church throughout the world. It is not enough for the bishops to be concerned about their own dioceses or even their national church. Through ordination, they become members of a group or college of bishops that, with and under the pope, has a shared responsibility for the universal church. One of the most important ways in which they fulfill that responsibility is by the contacts they develop with other bishops and the awareness they foster in their own churches of the concerns, challenges, and successes of Catholic communities all around the globe.

The papacy is clearly at the heart of Catholic unity. As the bishop of Rome, the pope has responsibilities analogous to those of other bishops. What gives his role its distinctive character is the conviction that as the successor of Peter he has a special role of leadership vis-à-vis the universal church. He is a bishop, but also more than just another bishop. He is in the college of bishops, but he is also its head. Although the pope's responsibilities are many and although, as we have seen, they touch on Catholic teaching and liturgy and institutional life, they all in some way come back to the theme of unity. The papacy exists in order above all to protect and foster Catholic unity.

Unity of faith and life have been a focus of concern for the church from the beginning. This chapter has tried to emphasize that such unity is not incompatible with diversity and that in the history of the church the balance between unity and pluralism has varied considerably. One of the distinctive features of the renewed vision of Catholicism that has come out of Vatican II has been its emphasis on the fact of pluralism and its value within the church. This presents the pope and the bishops with a new responsibility. They are not only to safeguard unity, but they are also to encourage a certain kind of pluralism. If the church is really going to be at home in all the different cultures of the world, if evangelization is to be an evangelization of cultures and national identities as well as of individuals, Catholic faith, liturgy, and life will have to find forms and patterns appropriate for different nations and regions. A failure to be open to a healthy pluralism in this regard can have as destructive an effect for the mission of the church as disunity and division.

Inculturation is clearly not an easy process, but it is a necessary one. In all its forms it involves risks and the real possibility of failure. One can fail here, however, not only by undermining unity but also by refusing to embrace necessary adaptations. Everyone in the church is called to contribute to the efforts that are required, especially those who have some competency in the areas under consideration as well as those in positions of authority. The function of the papacy here is both to foster pluralism and to see that it does not undermine unity. All churches need to deepen the awareness of their members that church life must always be lived out within the context of Catholic unity.

The idea of the universal church as a communion of churches has become increasingly popular in recent decades. Unity has nothing to do with uniformity, nor is it simply a matter of external control. Church unity is rooted in a unity of faith and love, of life and religious experience. It is rooted ultimately in the mysterious unity in plurality that is the inner life of the Trinity. The more profoundly local churches live in their own contexts out of the great and shared tradition of Catholic Christianity, the more readily will they recognize the bond that unites them to other churches and the more willingly will they work to ensure its continuing vitality.

The presence of the Holy Spirit in the church has been likened to that of a soul in a body. The Spirit is a source of life and energy and of creative activity. The Spirit of Christ is a Spirit of unity. The Spirit binds believers to Christ and to one another. At the same time the Spirit is a source of diversity. The Spirit, Paul taught, bestows a variety of gifts or charisms on all the faithful and, one might add by analogy, on individual churches. These gifts are not meant to divide the church but to enrich it. "To each is given the manifestation of the Spirit for the common good" (1 Cor 12:7). Pope and bishops serve both unity and diversity not by quenching the Spirit but rather by testing what is claimed to be done in the name of the Spirit and by encouraging and fostering what seems to be the result of the Spirit's inspiration.

CHAPTER SEVEN

Catholic Temptations and Catholic Renewal

Vatican II succeeded in bringing back to the consciousness of many Catholics the importance of the theme of reform and renewal. For centuries language of that kind had been all but identified with the Protestant Reformation and thus with a move- ment that, whatever the original intention of its leaders, ended by undermining the unity of the Western church. The tendency to identify talk of reform with Protestantism, as unjustified as it is in the light of history, helps to account for the surprise that many felt when a German cardinal in a speech at the council quoted an adage made famous by Martin Luther, *ecclesia semper reformanda est,* "the church always stands in need of reform."

One of the key terms that John XXIII used in formulating his own hopes for Vatican II was *aggiornamento.* The term sug- gests a bringing up to date, an adapting of church language, structures, and practices so that they might more adequately cor- respond to the experience of Catholics living in the modern world. The theme, for the pope, had nothing to do with superfi- cial changes or with any kind of easy compromise with values more or less incompatible with the gospel. For *aggiornamento,* as John XXIII understood it, to be successful, it would have to include a return to authentic Christian sources with the precise intention of deepening contemporary faith and religious life. The pope spoke of a new Pentecost, a new outpouring of the Spirit, that would renew the church and church members from within. At the same time he knew that the world and its various cultures were undergoing rapid and radical change. In order for Catholicism to play an active and dynamic role, it had to renew not only its inner life but the whole range of external forms in which that life was expressed.

Talk of *aggiornamento* presupposes an awareness of historicity, of the inevitable historical conditioning of all things human, including those that make up the life of the church. Such an awareness leads to the recognition of a need for adaptation, especially during periods of significant social and cultural change. As inevitable as such a task is for a historical community, it is rarely an easy one.

If the word *aggiornamento* points primarily to the historical character of the church, the language of reform evokes failure, inadequacy, and sinfulness. Individual Catholics, whether ordained or lay, whether members of religious communities or not, are constantly exposed to temptation and sin. Although this is always the case, history has known periods when the life of the church was marked by intense spiritual commitment and other periods when religious life was on the wane and when church leaders lived in ways that were radically at odds with the gospel message. In highlighting the image of the people of God, the bishops at Vatican II wanted to bring out not only the real humanity of the church but also the obvious fact that its members are sinners. The church is a community of sinners, a sinful church.

One of the traditional marks or characteristics of the church, according to the creed, is holiness. As the body of Christ animated by the Spirit, as a community of faith endowed with such gifts as the scriptures and the eucharist the church is truly holy. Individual Christians, moreover, through baptism share Christ's life, receive the gift of his Spirit, and become in a mysterious but true sense children of God. Paul described the Christians to whom he wrote as chosen and holy. At the same time he knew that they were capable of sin. The New Testament in its entirety bears witness to the small and large failings that marked the early church. If believers are holy, they are also called to become holy, to struggle against their weaknesses and failures and to form themselves more and more into the likeness of Christ. At the beginning of every eucharist, Catholics are invited to reflect on their sins and to ask for God's forgiveness.

Because all the baptized, from pope and bishops to religious and lay people, are exposed to sin and are in some sense sinners, all need to hear the call to conversion and to a renewed and deepened religious life. Such a call is rooted in the scriptures and over the centuries has been issued again and again by saints, preachers, church leaders, and church reformers. Most often it has been addressed to individuals, but it has also been directed to ecclesial communities and institutions and to the church itself. The need for corporate conversion was something that was emphasized at Vatican II. "The Church, however, clasping sinners to her bosom, at once holy and always in need of purification, follows constantly the path of penance and renewal" (*Dogmatic Constitution on the Church*, no. 8).

The need for reform, renewal, and *aggiornamento* flows from two basic facts. One is that the church is a church of free and weak human beings who as long as they live are exposed to sin and to inadequacies of various kinds. These effect them not only in their private lives but also in the role that they play in the church. At the same time, the church is a historical reality; it lives in and is molded by history. Its language, structures, liturgical forms, attitudes to the world—all aspects of church life—rooted as they are in the mystery of God turned to us in Christ and active in the world through the Spirit, bear the mark of time; they are influenced by the particular historical and cultural contexts within which they grew up and took their present forms. To that degree they need adaptation and renewal to make them effective within a changed historical situation. History, as well as human frailty, calls out for spiritual and institutional renewal.

If it is true that the realities and attitudes that have been evoked in earlier chapters are indeed characteristic of the Catholic experience of Christianity, then it seems natural to assume that they also represent areas and emphases in which Catholicism undergoes challenges and temptations that are somewhat distinctive of it. It is these rather than the more general temptations with which all believers have to struggle that constitute the focus of what follows.

COMMUNITY AND INDIVIDUAL

The Catholic emphasis on community inevitably leads to tensions and conflicts between the communal and especially the institutional elements in the church and individual church members. In the medieval and early modern periods, when the authority of the church was reinforced by the power of the state, this sometimes had disastrous results. Dissidents of various kinds were not only condemned and excommunicated by church leaders but were sometimes handed over to secular authorities for punishment and even execution. From a modern perspective of human dignity and individual rights, the activities of the Inquisition seem all but incomprehensible. In the context of the time they were often defended in terms of community rights including, above all, the right to maintain the purity of the truth of the gospel. This argument was only finally and officially repudiated at Vatican II with its document on freedom of religion.

In our own day a stress on the general norm, the ordinary pattern, the community celebration, can fail to do justice to the exception, to the person who does not, for whatever reason, easily fit into the group. This is increasingly becoming the situation of many Catholics in the contemporary North American church. Individualism has affected every aspect of life, including the religious. The answer here is not to make the community so closed that it would simply eliminate from it all who refused or were unable to fit into its life. The church here is obviously faced with a dilemma. On the one hand, without a real sense of community, without a shared faith and a common religious life, there really is no Catholicism. On the other hand, if church leaders draw the line too tightly or are incapable of a certain flexibility, they might well drive away people of genuine faith and commitment.

The present situation requires emphasis both on the value of community and on the rights and duties of individuals within it. The church could benefit in this regard from a deepened sense of the Spirit present and working within all the baptized. Vatican II appealed to the teaching of the apostle Paul in underlining the importance of the charisms that the Spirit has bestowed on all believers and that are meant to be put to the service of the common good. The challenge for church leaders is to encourage people to develop their gifts and talents and to find creative and imaginative ways of bringing them into the larger community. People need to be helped to rediscover the value of the religious community and to feel welcomed and at home in it. This will only be possible in a culture like ours if the community respects the individuals that make it up and strengthens and nurtures them in their individuality. Each person's religious journey is different. Not only that, it is a journey that has to pass through various stages. What is not possible today may be possible in the future. Patience is sometimes required on all sides.

The history of Catholicism is full of the stories of strong individuals, of people with distinctive gifts and an intensely personal religious life. To know anything about the lives of the saints is to know how different they were from one another and how often their efforts to renew religious orders or the broader community were met with suspicion and opposition. The only reason we know them as saints today is that they did not capitulate to such opposition but continued in their commitment to their own personal vision and to the church and its needs. Obvious examples here include such people as Francis of Assisi and Teresa of Avila, Ignatius of Loyola and Mary Ward.

By any standard, two of the greatest intellectual and religious figures in Catholic history were St. Augustine (354–430) and John Henry Cardinal Newman (1801–90). Both were strong individuals with a very developed sense of themselves and of the unique nature of their religious vocations. Augustine's *Confessions* has been one of the most influential books in the history of Western culture precisely because it bears witness to his extraordinary self-awareness, his acute insight into the complexity of his desires and fears, hopes and longings. The religious journey that took Augustine by such a round-about way to baptism and eventually to the responsibility of the episcopacy was a deeply personal one. Although he became progressively more conscious of the role of the church community, he never lost his sense of the intensely personal nature of the working of God's grace within him.

Newman also wrote an autobiography. Its form is somewhat different from that of Augustine, but it too reveals a person at the height of his powers, deeply conscious of the mysterious presence of God's guiding hand in his life. As Catholic as Newman genuinely was, he had a sense of a profoundly personal vocation. He spoke of "God and the self and of the self and God" as the key to his understanding of human life and of its ultimate meaning. In spite of the obvious individualism of such a vision, his whole career was marked by a deepening awareness of the importance of the community of faith. Having worked for years with his colleagues at Oxford and elsewhere for a renewal of the Catholic dimension of Anglicanism, he finally came to live Catholicism within the church of Rome. Even there, however, he maintained his appreciation for the individual and for individual conscience. He felt himself quite at odds with those Catholics who exaggerated the role of the pope and of the magisterium. He concluded the chapter on conscience in his 1874 "Letter to the Duke of Norfolk" with a sentence that has become famous: "If I am obliged to bring religion into after-dinner toasts,...I shall drink—to the pope, if you please—still, to conscience first, and to the pope afterwards."

Among the many distinguished representatives of the Catholic tradition that one might name, Newman and Augustine, as different as their historical and cultural contexts were from one another and from ours, are two remarkable examples of the kind of strong individuals that Catholicism over the centuries has been able to attract and make room for. They found their identities in no sense repressed but rather enhanced by the community of faith and by all the concrete things that life in it entailed. Even as they were strengthened by their membership in the church, they also served it with the extraordinary gifts of mind and heart that were theirs. Contemporary Catholicism will only thrive to the extent that it can continue to attract and maintain people of similar bent and to the extent that they will be able to put their gifts at its service. The Catholic emphasis on community is meant not to crush but to enhance individual gifts and talents.

BETWEEN PAST AND FUTURE

It is impossible for anyone who reflectively engages with Western culture to be unaware of Catholicism's presence in and influence on that culture over the centuries. A visit to Europe reveals its achievements in art and architecture at every turn. One of the highlights of my own student days in Germany was attending the world premiere of a deeply moving piece of contemporary religious music, the "Passion According to Luke," by the Polish composer Krzysztof Penderecki, in the cathedral at Münster, Westphalia. The building is late romanesque, early gothic. It has a certain rootedness, even a heaviness, that reflects the climate and the mentality of the Münsterland. In it are altars and works of art from the Renaissance and the Baroque periods. The main altar area has been tastefully redone to accommodate the renewed liturgy. The building and its furnishings bear witness to the living and developing tradition of Catholicism. The music that night could not have been more contemporary. It related the story of Jesus and his suffering and death to the passion of twentieth-century Europe. One could not help but think of the wars, the Holocaust, and the tragedy of what was still a divided continent. The contemporary music in that ancient architectural structure, itself restored after having been severely damaged in World War II, seemed to sing of a great and enduring religious tradition rooted in the past and open to the present.

When I spoke some time later with a local professor of theology about the sense of tradition that the cathedral gave me as a North American, he responded that for European Catholics such monuments are sometimes experienced as burdens, as things that threaten to close them off from contemporary issues and concerns. Tradition, he suggested, can be a source of identity and strength, but it can also become oppressive; it can condemn an individual or a community to live in the past.

Many North American Catholics could learn a great deal from the past achievements of the church, from its traditions of theology and prayer, of arts and religious life. They could also learn from the struggles of the popes and others to ensure the freedom of the church and to find ways of making it an effective force for justice in changing historical situations. On the other hand, some of those who are most committed to Catholic history and to Catholic tradition need to be aware of the temptation to focus so exclusively on the past that they are no longer open to the challenges of the present.

Catholic tradition is not static. Historical scholarship reveals how dynamic it has been in the past. That dynamism continues to be a law of its life. The church as an eschatological community is moving toward the future coming of God's kingdom, and part of its mission is helping to prepare for it. The very real responsibility that Catholics feel in regard to the past, in regard to what has been handed down in the tradition, as important as it is, should never blind them to God's call in the present.

An awareness of history can help keep an individual or an institution from responding precipitately to a new challenge. It can give a certain perspective, and that obviously is a positive thing. On the other hand, too great a preoccupation with the past can make one indifferent to pressing present problems. To know, for example, that the church in its history has lived through periods of decline and stagnation as well as periods of growth and vitality is no justification for failing to act here and now to the best of our ability. We have only one life, and each generation is asked to be responsible for its time and to help prepare the future that stands immediately before it. Cynicism about the limits of what human beings are able to achieve is not the same thing as commitment to tradition, even though it may present itself as such.

History and tradition are written into Catholic identity. They are sources of strength and renewal. To make them absolutes, however, to elevate them into exclusive norms of present attitudes and actions, is to succumb to a distinctively Catholic temptation. It is to undermine the present life of the church and impede it from fulfilling its pastoral responsibilities. Here as elsewhere balance is required.

FAITH AS ORTHODOXY AND AS PERSONAL RELIGIOUS EXPERIENCE

Faith is at the center of all Christian life. The Catholic tradition has put a particular emphasis on the content of faith—on the vision of God, the world, and human life that has been revealed through the person, teaching, and destiny of Jesus. At a very early date, and probably within the context of receiving converts into the community, this faith was articulated in the form of the creed. Debate about the meaning of various aspects of it led to synods and councils and to the attempt, at least in controverted areas, to establish a pattern of orthodoxy.

Concern for orthodoxy or right belief accounts for much that is distinctive of the Catholic tradition. It has been a particular focus of popes and bishops and has led to their being recognized as a teaching body in the church, the magisterium. The issue of orthodoxy and of the need for an ongoing development of the understanding of faith is a particular example of the tension between past and present that has already been evoked. Past dogmatic formulations, as authoritative and definitive as they are in themselves, do not provide answers to new questions, nor do they represent the best way of formulating the faith in a changed cultural context.

For the New Testament, faith is above all a living faith, a personal response to God's revelation in Christ. A one-sided emphasis on orthodoxy, especially on what might be called verbal orthodoxy—the simple ability to affirm the traditional language of the church—could lead to a lack of appreciation for the subjective dimension of faith. The way that individuals live their faith, the way that they appropriate it or make it their own, varies dramatically from person to person. It even varies within the life of a single person. Faith is not self-evident. It has always involved a risk, perhaps never more than in modern Western culture. To be a genuine believer today is not easy. Nor is it something that is resolved once and for all at any particular moment. People need to grow into their faith and learn to relate it to what is significant in their lives. To be able to recognize in the parables of Jesus and in the teaching of Paul, for example, one's own experience of faith is something that only comes after years of serious religious life.

A one-sided emphasis on verbal orthodoxy, on precise definitions and formulations of faith, could drive away people who have a genuine and living faith but who for whatever reasons are unable at this stage of their life to make the official language of the church their own. Preachers whose concern is only for orthodoxy tend to sound simplistic and/or rationalistic. They are certainly of little help to those struggling to relate traditional formulations to contemporary experience.

If the temptation of many people in the modern world is to disregard or to be indifferent to the "objective" nature of faith, the temptation in the Catholic tradition is to emphasize it to such a degree that people receive little help in understanding and growing into it. It almost becomes a test of ecclesial obedience. The Catholic understanding of faith offers a real corrective to certain contemporary trends, but for it to be effective it must be allied with a genuine respect for the spiritual journey of individuals. Preachers and teachers cannot be satisfied with simply repeating past formulations but must seek new and creative ways of drawing out their meaning so that people living today can understand and respond to them.

WORD AND SACRAMENT, PERSONAL PRAYER AND LITURGY

Chapter 4 attempted to suggest some of the human and spiritual riches that are contained in the traditional Catholic emphasis not only on the sacraments but on what has been called the sacramental principle. Protestant writers have sometimes accused Catholicism of being too all-embracing in this area, of trying to include in itself too much of what they see as forms of natural religiosity. The Protestant emphasis has tended to be on the word of God, the word of scriptures and of preaching, and on the individual's response of faith.

Vatican II implicitly recognized the validity of this critique and emphasized decisively the place of the word in the sacraments and in the whole of the liturgy. In spite of what the council had to say here, however, some traditional and some progressive elements in the church seem to continue to be more attracted to ritual and symbolism than to the scriptures or preaching. Obviously both elements are essential. Ritual clearly corresponds both to something deep in the human psyche and to the whole incarnational nature of God's saving activity. It is also a key means for building up a community and for handing on its values. At the same time the word has the ability to specify the ritual, to relate what otherwise might simply be archetypal to the historical person of Jesus and to his teaching and destiny. It can also personalize what is happening by relating it to the actual community gathered for the celebration.

The relative disregard of the scriptures and of preaching at certain periods in the church's history suggests that the traditional Catholic emphasis on sacraments can undermine the seriousness that the church and church leaders are to give to the word of God. An absolutely central value of Christianity in itself, the word of God offers a corrective to a variety of temptations to which a sacramental religion is exposed. Liturgy and sacraments are in no sense self-justifying. Even the act of worship demands a corresponding life on the part of worshipers. The function of the word here is to stimulate believers to a personal response in faith to the ritual and to challenge them to translate what they celebrate into everyday life. If the eucharist does not deepen people's life of discipleship, then it is to some degree failing in its purpose.

The liturgical renewal that came out of Vatican II was largely inspired by the practice of the early church and has given expression to many values that were central to it. The present liturgy, whatever its inadequacies, is a remarkable embodiment of much that is essential to Catholicism. It emphasizes the communal as well as the sacramental nature of the Catholic faith. A temptation that could arise here would be to insist on maintaining particular forms of ritual simply because they were developed in the ancient church. As conservative by nature as good ritual is, it cannot cease to undergo a certain development lest it become little more than a museum piece. The balance is not easy to find. If it is foolish to jettison traditional forms in an attempt to be resolutely contemporary, it is equally wrong to insist that religious ritual and symbolism, art and music, must be totally out of step with what is best in contemporary culture.

Another temptation to which some Catholics might be exposed in this area is to overemphasize the communal aspect of liturgical celebrations to the point that they end up by at least indirectly undermining the value of personal prayer and personal devotion. Both are important. Personal prayer is part of an individual's faith journey. Without it, moreover, the liturgy itself could rapidly be emptied of its inner content. It could become mere ritual that does not find in one's heart and life the echo that it is meant to have.

HIERARCHY AND COMMUNITY, AUTHORITY AND SERVICE

The hierarchy and the ordained ministry continue to play a crucial role in Catholicism. As positive as their role over the centuries has been, church leaders, like everyone else in the community of faith, are exposed to a variety of temptations, some of which are intimately connected to their office. In the past, when the church was wealthier and had a much more significant place in society than today, these temptations often had to do with power and privilege. Even now the priesthood or the episcopate might seem to some a way of exercising a kind of spiritual power over others. Perhaps a more common temptation at the present time, given the challenges facing the church, is for the clergy to withdraw into a world of their own, a world that is different from and insensitive to that of the vast majority of lay Catholics.

A difficult question that faces and will continue to face Catholicism in the years to come has to do with the conditions for ordination. Who should be ordained? It is here that the debates about celibacy and the ordination of women are to be located. The official teaching about the ordination of women to the priesthood has already been spelled out; it is that the pope and bishops are incapable, for doctrinal reasons, of modifying the present practice. The question of a married clergy is and will always be a more open one. It is a matter of church law or discipline, exceptions to which are made from time to time. Those who believe, for example, that present pastoral needs call for the ordination of married people as well as celibates see the hierarchy as tempted to continue a traditional practice for fear of the risk that a significant change like this would entail. The opposite attitude sees the suggestion of a modification of the present law as a temptation to abandon authentic Catholic values in the face of present and perhaps passing attitudes and mentalities. There is no simple solution here. Everyone involved needs to continue to seek the guidance of the Spirit and the courage to embrace and carry out what finally seems to be God's will for the church at this moment of its history.

The hierarchy is not the church. In fact, as Cardinal Newman once commented, the clergy would look rather foolish without the lay people. Vatican II has brought back to Catholic consciousness the importance of the whole people of God. All the baptized receive the gift of the Spirit and have a real share in Christ's priesthood. All are called to an active role in the life and mission of the church. This renewed emphasis on the whole community entails a shift in the way Catholics are invited to think about ecclesiastical office. It is a ministry, a service, situated within the church and with a responsibility to help build it up. The new vision of Vatican II, taken together with the significant decline in recent years in the number of priests and religious, offers a clear indication that Catholicism is undergoing a profound change in this area. Less emphasis will be given in the future to the ordained ministry and more to the laity. In the interim, this means a special challenge for both hierarchy and laity.

The post-conciliar era has shown that it is not easy to shift from an experience of the church focused on the ordained to one in which all the faithful are to take more active roles. It has not been easy for many of the ordained to modify how they see their role, nor has it been easy for lay people to respond to the new challenges and opportunities that have been presented to them. In fact, as the years have gone by, one has the impression that some priests and bishops, in spite of the obvious practical motives that exist for involving lay people in new roles in parish and dioceses, have in fact more or less abandoned the effort to do so. The reaction is understandable and reflects a typically Catholic temptation. The institutional element of the church is so entrenched and in certain ways so effective that simply running it has come for many to be an alternative to the more difficult task of inspiring, educating, and involving the laity in new ministries.

The hierarchy and the ordained ministry will always be central to Catholic Christianity. Like everyone else, Catholic priests and bishops will continue to have temptations related to their responsibilities. Perhaps the most effective means they have to struggle against them is the biblical notion of church office as ministry or service. To be ordained is not to receive some kind of gift or honor for oneself. One is ordained for others, for God and Christ, and also for the community of faith. Ordination involves real leadership, but it is a leadership of service within a community of faith all of whose members are called to Christian maturity and to co-responsibility for the well-being of the whole church. The temptation not to take seriously the gifts of others, not to believe in their Christian dignity, needs constantly to be fought against. The words of Jesus in Luke's account of the last supper are a promise and a warning: "But I am among you as one who serves" (Lk 22:27).

UNITY NOT UNIFORMITY, DIVERSITY NOT DIVISION

One of the great strengths of the Catholic tradition has been its unity. In the modern period unity tended increasingly to be seen as uniformity. Vatican II, while in no sense wanting to undermine unity, sought to open the church again to the values of diversity. In doing so it was inspired by the example of the patristic church and by the witness of so many bishops at the council from different parts of the globe. The universality to which the very word *catholic* points implies pluralism. Catholic unity needs to be understood and practiced in ways that do not undermine legitimate diversity but rather enhance it. There is a strength in diversity as well as in unity.

The post-conciliar period has shown how difficult it is to find a balance between basically complementary but sometimes conflicting values. Talk of catholicity and of pluralism led to a considerable emphasis being given in some countries to the national church and to the need for distinctive liturgical and other forms. The key challenge for many became inculturation. Such developments provoked a reaction on the part of other Catholics, including bishops, in Rome and elsewhere, who saw in what was being done a danger to Catholic unity. It is not always easy to judge when adaptation has gone too far or when it has not gone far enough. This is particularly true in regard to formulations of faith and liturgical practices both of which have levels of meaning and implications that go beyond the obvious. The contemporary Catholic temptation in this area is twofold. On the one hand, some are tempted to protect the value of unity at all costs, even to the point of undermining the church's efforts at evangelization in changing and diverse cultures. Carried to an extreme this could prevent a healthy and necessary inculturation of the gospel in non-European continents. On the other hand, a real commitment to pastoral needs and to a desire to make the gospel and Catholic life relevant to local cultures is exposed to the danger of losing sight of something essential, of breaking at a very deep level the bond of unity that is so central to the Catholic experience of Christianity.

That these opposite temptations confront the church today and that different people within it tend to be more exposed to one or the other of them should not be too surprising. It says something about Catholic fullness. There is such a range of values in the church that no one person and no one period could embody them all in a way that would be valid for everyone and for all time. The church, as individuals, lives in history and is therefore exposed to the risks of history. It is constantly confronted with new challenges, new situations. Decisions need to be taken, whether about theological formulations or ritual practices or new structures for institutional and community life. In almost every case several values have to be weighed. Sometimes what should be done is relatively clear; at other times it is much less so. In the latter cases people tend to fall back on what for them are primary concerns, whether unity or adaptation. What is important is that people on both sides of the divide recognize the particular temptation to which they are exposed and that they try to appreciate the values embraced by the other group.

The phenomenon of the almost opposite temptations toward division or uniformity is indicative of the complex situation of Catholicism within contemporary Western culture. There is clearly scope here for adaptation and openness and for a willingness to dialogue with the genuine values of our time, including its heightened sense of personal dignity. At the same time, much that is best and most authentic in the Catholic tradition is, at least superficially, at odds with much of modern culture, beginning with its sense of God and of grace and continuing with its emphasis on community, tradition, and hierarchy. The real contribution the church has to make to modernity and the things that will attract people to it will be precisely those aspects of its tradition that complement modernity, that make up for and offer a way of overcoming its inadequacies.

The Catholic values and emphases to which earlier chapters have drawn attention both define the distinctively Catholic and suggest the contribution the church has to make to contemporary society. For it to do so, more and more of its members will have to be exposed to these values and come to appreciate the ways in which they enhance our human and religious lives. As great a challenge as that is, there is another one. Committed and aware Catholics need to foster their identity in such a way as to be open to and welcoming toward people of the present time. What are real strengths in the church and its tradition should not be turned into caricatures of themselves by exaggeration.

The use of words like *conservative* and *progressive* to describe individuals and groups within the post-conciliar church has become relatively common. Such terms are not always helpful. Catholicism to some degree is and must be both progressive and conservative. It is rooted in and celebrates and tries to live out of Jesus Christ and what it was that God did for the world through his life, death, and resurrection. Nor can one simply disregard all that has happened between his time and ours. The Spirit of Christ has been with the church on its historical pilgrimage and has helped it to develop understandings and lifestyles from which we can continue to learn. On the other hand, history continues. The challenge today as in the past is to proclaim the gospel to new generations of people and to do it in terms of the culture within which they live. The church is both old and new. It is turned to the past and to the future. It lives out of an extraordinary fullness that permits it at one time to stress this element and at another, that. If it is to fulfill its mission, it can neither cut itself off from its origins and its past nor close itself to the ever new present through which alone it can pass into the future. Although individual Catholics may be more progressive or more conservative, the church as such needs to be both.

A TRADITION OF CATHOLIC REFORM

The need of Catholics throughout their lives to be called to personal renewal and personal conversion is something that is reflected in the liturgical year with its season of Lent and with the renewal of baptismal promises as a part of the Easter celebration. Traditional Catholic practices like retreats and parish missions and days of recollection are all meant to serve the same purpose. The focus in the present section is not on these things, as important as they are, but rather on examples from history of attempts to renew the church itself. Efforts in this direction became increasingly common in the medieval period when a whole rhetoric having to do with the reformation of the church and of religious life developed.

In the Catholic tradition monasticism and religious orders have repeatedly presented themselves as instruments of church renewal. If the motive behind the first monks who went out into the desert of Egypt in the late third century to pursue a life of prayer and asceticism was personal sanctification, it was not long before some of them began forming monastic communities. Whatever their intention in doing so, their community life soon began to act as a stimulus and an instrument of reform within the broader church. St. Basil of Caesarea, one of the founders of Christian monasticism, was inspired in his rule by the ideal of the church life described in the Acts of the Apostles. He saw the monastic community as trying to live the Christian life to a certain degree of intensity and in doing so as challenging the church around it to renew and deepen its life. Somewhat of the same idea was developed by St. Augustine in his writings on monastic life and in the actual community he formed around himself in Hippo.

In the early medieval period monasteries became centers of learning and culture as well as of prayer and liturgy. When monasticism itself began to lose its ideals and fell into the hands of secular lords, it was a monastery, that of Cluny, that initiated a reform movement that ended by renewing not only monastic life but the religious life of the papacy and of the whole Western church. Its efforts flowed into what is known as the Gregorian reform, a reform movement centered on the papacy that extended throughout the last half of the eleventh and into the early part of the twelfth century. It is named after the pope who played the most dominant role in it, Gregory VII (1074–85). A number of the popes involved in the renewal were themselves monks, including some who came from Cluny. The reform had both a personal and an institutional dimension to it. The great moral issues for the clergy at the time had to do with simony and with concubinage. The reformers were committed to the value of celibacy and took every possible measure to ensure its observance. Simony has to do with the buying and selling of church offices, including the office of bishop and of abbot. The obvious danger here was that unworthy candidates would buy their way into such positions in order to benefit from the power or wealth attached to them. The institutional issue had to do with the role of the emperor in the naming and appointing of bishops and of their responsibilities to him. The debate focused on lay investiture, the ritual act by which the emperor invested bishops with the insignia of their office. The struggle between pope and emperor was long and difficult but was eventually won by the papacy. The result was a heightened emphasis on the papal role in church and society and a greater freedom of church structures and offices from secular control.

The Gregorian reform, widely recognized as one of the really decisive turning points in Catholic history, brought about a genuine and long-lasting renewal of church life. Although it was rooted in and helped in a variety of ways by the monastic reform of Cluny, it eventually became a reform that was led by the papacy. It is perhaps the most famous example in church history of Catholic reform being carried out by the pope himself.

The Protestant Reformation in the early sixteenth century was as successful as it was because of the widespread sense of a need for reform that existed in European society at the time. Religious and church life in the fifteenth century was clearly in a state of decline at both the individual and the institutional levels. Throughout the period people from a wide range of backgrounds and walks of life raised the cry for reform of the church "in head and members." The very success of the Protestant reformers bears witness to the fact that there were already elements at work seeking to reverse the general decline. Many such elements existed in Spain and in Italy and they along with other factors would eventually give rise to the Counter or Catholic Reformation, the renewal of the church that subsequently came to be related in a special way with the work of the council of Trent.

The Catholic Reformation was fed from below by the renewal of existing forms of religious life and by the founding of new orders such as the Capuchins and the Jesuits. Various other groups and movements became convinced of the need for personal and ecclesial renewal and gradually developed, among other things, a more pastoral and more spiritual image of the bishop. Charles Borromeo became the archbishop of Milan and in his exercise of his office embodied the ideal of the reformed Catholic episcopate. Although the council of Trent largely focused in its doctrinal statements on the challenge represented by the theological positions of Luther, it also issued a number of practical and pastoral decrees that called for, among other things, a renewal of preaching and of the liturgy and for the setting up of seminaries throughout the Catholic world. Although the popes were not initially in the forefront of the Catholic Reformation, they did endorse the work of Trent and became the major instruments in its implementation.

VATICAN II AS A COUNCIL OF RENEWAL

Even a cursory overview of history suggests that concern for renewal and reform has often been a priority in Catholic consciousness and that at various times different individuals and groups within the church have played key parts in bringing it about. Individual saints like Catherine of Siena, Bernard of Clairvaux, or Teresa of Avila exercised roles not unlike those of the classical biblical prophets. They attacked abuse at whatever level it existed and called for personal and institutional reform. Individual monasteries and religious communities also played their part, as did councils and popes. In the case of Charlemagne, crowned emperor by the pope in 800, and his successors, lay and secular leaders became involved in the inner life of the church and were instrumental in working for its reform.

Vatican II was a council of renewal. It called individual Catholics, lay, religious, and ordained, to personal conversion and to a more authentic Christian discipleship and at the same time attempted to renew the church in almost all aspects of its community and institutional life. The latter efforts presupposed an awareness of two things. On the one hand, with the passage of time certain features of church life had lost something of their vitality or had developed in one-sided ways that needed to be counterbalanced. On the other hand, the council was sensitive to the changes that had taken and were taking place in Western culture and throughout the world and saw in them a challenge to the church to develop new and imaginative ways of adapting itself to the changed situation.

The documents of Vatican II did not descend ready made from heaven, nor was their content created out of nothing by the bishops during the four short years that the council was in session. They were able to build on and to carry further a process of renewal that had already been underway for several decades. The liturgical movement offers an excellent example. Although some scholars seek its roots in the nineteenth century and in certain innovations made by Pius X, the twentieth-century liturgical movement received its initial major impulse in the 1910s and 1920s from a number of Benedictine monasteries in Belgium and Germany. Before long individual priests with pastoral responsibilities in various European countries and especially in France became involved in it and gave it a more popular direction. Meetings and conferences in the years after World War II won adherents to the movement among both laity and clergy throughout Europe and in North America. Pius XII in a 1947 encyclical, *Mediator Dei,* recognized its importance and gave it an initial endorsement and in the 1950s introduced changes in the Holy Week celebrations recommended by it.

The liturgical movement was parallelled by other movements focused on theology, scripture studies, ecumenism, and the lay apostolate. All of these movements at one time or another ran into difficulty with church authorities. They seemed to some to be too progressive, too critical of past practices, too open to the world and to modern scholarship. Gradually, however, they won acceptance until at Vatican II much that was central to them was taken over and made part of the official teaching and practice of the church.

Without all the work and experimentation that had preceded it, the council would not have been able to achieve what it did; what it finally did achieve, however, cannot be reduced to a simple endorsement of what others had done before it. The council was a significant and creative event in itself. It brought together bishops from all over the world and provided them with an opportunity to discuss and debate a variety of issues related to the church—to its inner life, its relation to other religious groups, its mission in the modern world. In spite of conflicts and differences of opinion among them, the vast majority of the bishops came to recognize and accept that they were participants in a massive process of renewing the whole life of the church. They were grateful for what had been done in the years leading up to the council and turned to many of the theologians and others who had contributed to that earlier process to help them in their deliberations. What they produced in the end, however, remains very much their work and their responsibility. They offered a vision of a renewed Catholicism and laid down certain guidelines for its implementation.

As a council of renewal, Vatican II's ultimate significance will be established only over time as its decrees and its call for change in attitudes and structures become part of the life of the church. The initial process of implementation turned out in some ways to be more difficult than many had anticipated. For some clergy and religious it provoked a crisis of identity.

Renewing the Catholic Church, effecting *aggiornamento* in regard to so many aspects of its life and self-understanding, has not been an easy task. This should not be surprising, given the size of the church and the fact that it exists in such different situations around the globe. Moreover, Vatican II followed a period in church history when relatively little change was made, which made renewal all the more difficult. Acknowledging all of this, one has to recognize that the extent of the renewal that has been brought about is quite remarkable.

Vatican II, like other historically significant efforts at church reform, called for renewal of mind and heart as well as of institutions and structures. As important as the latter are, without the

former they remain superficial and without real spiritual significance. The renewal of the liturgy that the bishops were seeking,
for example, was not going to be achieved by simply developing
new rituals and translating them into the vernacular. It required a
profound renewal on the part of all Catholics, lay and ordained,
regarding understanding of and attitude toward the liturgy and
their role in it. Such renewal demands a real process of education
and of spiritual growth, which are much more difficult to bring
about than the writing of a new ritual.

TEMPTATIONS AND RENEWAL

Made up of morally and spiritually weak and vulnerable
human beings, the church is exposed in all its members to sin of
every kind. The need to struggle against and overcome such sinfulness is a never-ending one. As a community of faith with its own
distinctive characteristics, Catholicism is exposed to temptations
that in many cases arise from carrying positive Catholic values to
an extreme. Both leaders and people need to be on their guard
against such tendencies and to seek ways of preventing them.

Ecclesia semper reformanda est–the church needs always to be
undergoing renewal and reform. The impulse for such a process
can come from the grassroots or from religious orders or from
the hierarchy. Authentic Catholic reform will always at some
point include all three of these elements and more. Vatican II
represents a special instance in Catholic history of a council committed to wide-ranging renewal. Although it has already borne a
great deal of fruit, its legacy is far from exhausted. As the church
faces a new millennium, its documents, its vision, and its spirit
continue to offer a beacon and a model for the continuing
renewal that Catholicism always requires. For many people, Vatican II brought back a sense of the breadth and depth of the
Catholic tradition and revealed its capacity to stimulate and ani-
mate a new and creative period in church history.

CHAPTER EIGHT

Being Catholic Today

Up this point I have tried to suggest some of the distinctive characteristics of Catholicism and of its liturgical, intellectual, and institutional life. Of necessity, much has remained general, even abstract. The features that have been touched on, however, do belong to the Catholic tradition and as such to some degree influence the experience of individual Catholics even when they are more or less unaware of them.

This final chapter focuses more directly on the experience of the individual Catholic. In one sense, what I am proposing to do here is impossible. Catholics experience their religion in a wide variety of ways. We are all individuals with distinctive ethnic, cultural, educational, and religious backgrounds. We have different experiences of life, of its good things but also of its trials and difficulties. And yet as Catholics there are things that we share. So, while recognizing the inevitable inadequacy and one-sidedness of what follows, I would like to suggest how a relatively self-aware and reflective Catholic living in contemporary North American society might experience his or her religion.

OUR COMMON HUMANITY

The person I have in mind in writing this chapter is an adult of whatever age who might be going through or have recently gone through the RCIA program. It might be a young person who was baptized a Catholic as an infant and who has begun to reflect seriously on his or her religion. It might be an older person who for years has lived her or his faith but who now feels drawn to reflect on it more consciously in order to deepen it and to live it more fully.

Like everyone else, Catholics begin and end with the simple fact of their humanity. We are all human beings; we are born and grow and undergo an enormous variety of experiences and, in the end, have to confront and deal with sickness and death. Because we live today and because we live in North America we experience all of these things in ways that are different from the ways in which our forebears experienced them, different too from the ways in which people in other parts of the globe experience them. The fundamental human realities remain, but the precise manner in which we live them is inevitably influenced by the social-cultural context in which we find ourselves.

To some degree our lives focus on ourselves—our joys and pleasures, pains and sorrows, hopes and fears, successes and failures. But our lives also involve others. We are children of our parents, and in many cases we have sisters and brothers and other relatives. We relate to other people; we fall in love, we develop friendships, we get married. Many of us begin the cycle all over again by having our own children. Most of us have a sense of right and wrong, of good and evil. We want to do something positive with our life; we want to make some kind of contribution to what is larger than ourselves, to what is called the common good. We rejoice when the world around us seems to be working—when the poor and the vulnerable are helped and when people we know are able to find work and to provide for their families.

We all experience human failure, including moral failure. People hurt one another and become involved in self-destructive behavior; children are abused; women are treated violently; families break down. Public figures sometimes act in ways that are manifestly disreputable and in doing so reinforce a tendency in many of us to cynicism. There is no escaping the great social and economic struggles and confrontations of the world and of our own communities. Much of public life seems to be driven by selfishness, greed, and blind ambition. On the other hand, we all experience positive things as well. We see instances of parental love for young children, of dedication between spouses, of supportive fidelity among friends. Science, technology, music, and art enrich our lives and in the process reveal something of the wonderfully creative capacities that are ours as human beings.

There is nothing in all this that is foreign to Catholicism. It recognizes and rejoices in what is good and positive and uplifting about our lives; it is equally realistic about what is negative and destructive in them. To be a Christian and a Catholic does not involve a turning of our back on our humanity or that of others but rather an understanding and living of it in all its dimensions.

One of our more distinctive characteristics as human beings is that we find ourselves from time to time wondering about who and what we are and about the meaning of our lives and of the life of the world. We wonder about the reality of good and evil and how in our own lives they interact; we ponder what we can do to become the kind of persons that we intuitively sense we are called to be. Such wonder inevitably leads to the question of God. Is there something or someone other than and beyond the vast cosmos that science has progressively opened up for us, something or someone that grounds and gives meaning to all that is? Does the world, do we, make sense in and of ourselves? Is what we know through our ordinary experience and through science all there is, or does our experience itself point to what lies beyond such realms to a level of reality that is totally other and yet somehow accounts for our world? Much of humanity since its origins and until today has answered this last question in the affirmative. In different languages and images human beings have recognized God as the creator, the ground, the beginning and the end, the universal Father, the companion of our journey, the holy Mystery that surrounds and permeates and gives meaning to our lives.

THE BIBLICAL GOD

Catholicism is above all a religion. Central to everything about it—to its faith, its ritual and its institutional life—is the reality of God. Religion is a many-sided phenomenon and as such has an impact on various aspects of individual and social life. One can study it from a historical or cultural or sociological point of view. As religion, however, what it affirms and what it wants to serve and foster more than everything else is a vision and an experience of God. The Catholic Church has often found itself at odds with aspects of modern culture, whether Western capitalist and consumer-oriented materialism or Marxism, because they have attempted to affirm a comprehensive vision of human life and of the world that denies the reality or at least the significance of God.

An authentic religious life only begins to develop in a serious way when a person becomes aware of his or her longing and capacity for God and tries to be sensitive and responsive to them. For Christianity, God does not remain hidden and in darkness. Freely and lovingly and in order to invite us into relationship, God has revealed something of the divine in the story of Israel and especially in the person and destiny of Jesus. The God of the Bible is both the God of creation and the Lord of human history. In the story of the exodus and of the covenant, God is manifested as a God of liberation and of salvation. The biblical God hears the cry of the poor and comes to their rescue. Moses and the prophets, the psalmists and the authors of the various books of wisdom, teach the people of Israel about their God and about the way of life that they are called to embrace. They are to praise and worship God and to keep the covenant that God has made with them. They are to obey God's commandments and to live in holiness of life.

For Christians, the biblical God has become manifest in a new and definitive way in the life and destiny of Jesus. More than that, in Jesus, especially in his death and resurrection, God is revealed as actively present in the midst of human history offering us forgiveness and the possibility of a new and renewed moral and religious life. The evangelist John, in both his gospel and letters, sums up the mystery of God as revealed and communicated in Jesus in terms of love. God so loved the world that he sent his only Son and the Son so loved us that he gave himself for our salvation. "Whoever has seen me has seen the Father" (Jn 14:9). "This is my commandment, that you love one another as I have loved you" (Jn 15:12). "Everyone who loves is born of God and knows God...for God is love" (1 Jn 4:7–8).

If a serious religious life begins with a sense of God, a specifically Christian life is rooted in the conviction that Jesus is the human face of God. He proclaims God's word and teaches God's wisdom. More than that, he is the divine Wisdom and Word incarnate. Everything he was and did revealed God and God's saving intention in our regard. The way that Jesus reached out to those who were suffering, to the woman with the running sore, to the widow with her dead son; the fact that he ate with publicans and sinners; the way that he welcomed children; the compassion that led him to feed the hungry: all these things reveal God and God's attitudes and concerns. In calling God Abba, Father, Jesus emphasized not the masculine nature of God but the intimacy of his relationship to God. In teaching us the Our Father, Jesus was inviting us to enter into and share that same relationship with him.

At the heart of Christian faith and Christian life is the paschal mystery, the saving reality of the death and resurrection of Jesus. The suffering and death of Jesus reveal on the one hand the depth of his love and fidelity and on the other the power of sin and evil and the tendency of the world and people to reject God's offer of salvation. God's raising of Jesus to the fullness of life affirms that his ministry and sacrifice have been accepted and have become a means of universal reconciliation. The death and resurrection together constitute a single, saving event. The nature of God's intention on our behalf has been revealed in this event in a new way. In the resurrection of Jesus God makes manifest our destiny and that of the world. In spite of sin and self-destructiveness and every kind of evil, God has not abandoned creation but in and through Christ has brought about its salvation. Although that salvation will only reach its fulfillment in the future, it has begun even now. The paschal mystery is completed by the gift of the Spirit. The risen Christ continues to be present in the world and in the hearts of believers through the Holy Spirit, who is poured out on all who have faith in Christ.

For Christians, the holy Mystery, the creator God, the Lord of history, is inseparable from Jesus, who through his resurrection has been revealed as Christ and Lord, as the Son and Word of God incarnate. Jesus is inseparable from the Holy Spirit, who has always been present in the world and in human history but who now resides in a special way in the church and in the hearts of believers as the Spirit of the risen Christ. Catholicism affirms, not just as an abstract article of faith but as the dynamic ground of our religious lives, the reality of God as a saving mystery of Father, Son, and Spirit. God is not only the creator but also the one who came into our world as our savior; God remains among us as the source and inspiration of our religious and human lives.

LIVING IN THE PRESENCE OF GOD

To be a Catholic is, at the deepest level, to live life in relation to and in communion with God. Because of Jesus we know that God is not distant but near, we know that through the gift of the Spirit, God is, as it were, in all the fullness of the divine life, alive and active in our hearts, calling us into relationship. If life is a journey, then God is our companion on the journey. If we are made for love and joy, for truth and beauty, then God is the one who will one day fulfill our capacity and longing even as here and now God gives us a foretaste of that fulfillment.

To use a traditional image, we are fish and God is the ocean. In God, Acts says, we live and move and have our being (Acts 17:28). St. Paul was so convinced that Christ was in him and that he was in Christ that he cried out on one occasion, "For to me, living is Christ" (Phil 1:21). In the high priestly prayer of John's gospel Jesus assures us that those who love him and keep his word will be loved by God and that Jesus and the Father will dwell in them (Jn 14:23).

God is present with us at every moment of our lives, at every step of our journey. God's presence means acceptance and forgiveness, strength and courage, trust and hope. As we grow in faith, we grow in our sensitivity to that presence. It bursts upon us in a special way at key moments of our life. To experience the meaning of moral responsibility, to perform a genuinely selfless act, to recognize the grace of being loved, to marvel at human creativity, to confront death: such moments can be occasions for a deeply personal experience of the reality of God. Most of us have such experiences. Having them within a context of Catholic prayer and liturgy helps us to recognize them for what they are.

As much as God is present to the whole of our life, we need from time to time and in an explicit way to reflect on God's presence, to try to respond to it, to find words to express the silent dialogue that is unfolding within and around us. Prayer is critical to a religious life. It is at the heart of being a Catholic. Prayer takes many forms; it passes through various stages. What seems to work at one time is unfruitful at another. What occasionally is simple and straightforward can sometimes demand a real effort.

Put most simply, prayer is being aware of God alive and active in us. People speak of entering into the presence of God. The challenge is not to go in search of God as one far away, but rather to attune ourselves to ourselves and to the divine presence in us. Saints often draw analogies between prayer and conversation with a friend. Sometimes we talk a great deal, we ask questions, we pour out our feelings, we recount what we have been doing. At other times we are delighted simply to be together. A rich form of prayer is the prayer of simple presence. We become conscious of God in us and try to remain quietly and calmly open to the divine presence. To be aware of God in this way is to be aware of our own roots and depths and mystery. Although we often find ourselves tossed about on the surface of life—fulfilling this responsibility, meeting that emergency, worrying about elderly parents or children or an unhappy spouse—prayer makes us aware of our own inner depths and of how they open out onto the infinite mystery of God.

The prayer of simple presence does not come easily; it requires real discipline and takes time. We need to feed it with other forms of prayer. Jesus himself taught us to use words when we pray. His prayer life was nurtured by the great tradition of Israel and especially by the psalms. In them we hear every kind of emotion being poured out before God. Their authors praise and worship and thank God and cry out for help in their need. The psalms teach us that we should not hesitate to give voice before God to our pain and anxiety, to lament the evil that we and God's world continue to suffer. The psalms draw us beyond lament to trust and hope. They teach us to pray for deliverance and for help of every kind. Jesus summed up much of the wisdom of the psalms in the Our Father, the greatest of all Christian prayers. We are invited to speak directly to God, to think of God as a loving and tender parent, to enter with Jesus into the intimacy that he had with God. We begin by praying that God's name will be hallowed, that God will be recognized as God and praised and worshiped and that God's will for us and for the world will be carried out. Prayer begins with God. But it also concerns us and our needs. We pray for our daily bread, for our everyday needs, and for forgiveness and help in the continuing struggle to lead a good life.

The Our Father is in itself an enormously rich prayer; we will never exhaust its meaning. It is also a model and pattern of what is involved in all authentic prayer. To recite it reflectively is not only to say a prayer but to dispose oneself for other forms of prayer and especially for the prayer of simple presence.

BELONGING TO GOD'S FAMILY

One of the more creative and important results of the recent liturgical renewal has been the development of the new Rite of Christian Initiation of Adults (RCIA), which we discussed briefly in chapter 4. The RCIA emphasizes the communal nature of Catholicism. In our search for God and in our efforts to try to lead a religious and spiritual life, we are not alone. For some this sense of the corporate nature of Catholicism is reinforced by the fact that their families and large numbers of people sharing their ethnic background are Catholic. For others this is much less the case. With the increasingly secular and pluralistic nature of North American society, being a practicing Catholic has become much more of a voluntary phenomenon. This does not mean simply choosing to believe in Catholic doctrine and to follow Catholic moral teaching; rather, it involves a free and deliberate decision to become an active member of a parish or of some other worshiping community. Membership in such a community works in two ways. On the one hand, it is meant to help us as individual believers, to strengthen us, to contribute to the nourishing and reinforcing of our Christian life. On the other hand, it entails responsibilities. Being a Catholic means participating actively in the life of the church. This obviously involves a participation in the liturgy, but it also includes active participation in the mission of the church. Such participation can take many forms and will certainly vary in intensity over the course of a person's life. Over the years various movements and groups have developed that have helped people to deepen their sense of belonging and provided them with an outlet for community activity. One need only think of the St. Vincent de Paul Society, various youth groups and ministries, parish catechetical programs, social-justice groups, or the pro-life movement. More and more parishes are creating prayer as well as study and action groups, all of which in their different ways enable recent converts and lifelong Catholics to find ways to have their communal sense of their religion nourished and to exercise in some concrete form their own community responsibility.

A parish that commits itself to developing an RCIA program and to all that such a program presupposes and entails cannot help but renew the Christian and community sense of all its members. The involvement of sponsors and catechists as well as the public rites marking the various stages of the program and especially the corporate celebration of the sacraments of initiation at the Easter Vigil remind parishioners of the deeply religious and communitarian nature of their own baptism. Lent in such parishes is experienced as a time of deepening conversion and of genuine renewal. The reaffirmation of baptismal commitments within the community at Easter can be a moment to recognize anew all that is implied in an authentic Christian and Catholic life.

A EUCHARISTIC COMMUNITY

The RCIA emphasizes the unity that is meant to exist among the sacraments of initiation. Through baptism and confirmation we are plunged into the death and resurrection of Jesus and are anointed with the gift of the Pentecostal Spirit. Christ and the Holy Spirit mutually reinforce one another. The coming of Christ has resulted in a new outpouring of God's Spirit on us. The Spirit, in turn, unites us to Christ and to other believers. If the church is the body of Christ, the Spirit is the source of its inner life.

As truly as baptism and confirmation unite us with Christ and the Spirit and bring us into the community of faith, the

meaning of membership in that community finds its most elo-
quent expression in the eucharist. The RCIA underlines in a new
way that the Mass or the eucharist is at the heart of Catholic
Christianity. Participation in it marks the culmination of the initiation process. Catholics have always put a great emphasis on
the Mass even when it was celebrated in a language that most
people did not understand and in a way that emphasized the role
of the clergy.

At the heart of the recent liturgical renewal has been the
conviction that the liturgy and especially the Mass are not things
that the clergy do for people but rather acts of the whole community of faith. The eucharist is an act of the church. We gather
as a community and together with the priest praise and worship
God and seek God's blessing on our lives. Most of the recent
changes in the liturgy have been intended to facilitate a conscious and active participation by all.

Sunday and the eucharist have been central to Catholic life
from its very beginning. The first Christians were Jews and continued to keep the sabbath, but very early they began marking
Sunday in a special way as the day of the resurrection. It was also
the first day of the week and as such suggested the beginning of a
new creation. To underline the newness that Sunday represented, they sometimes called it the eighth day. The eucharist
celebrates what for Paul and the whole of the tradition after him
is the heart of Christian faith, the paschal mystery, the saving
event represented by the death and resurrection of Jesus. There
could not have been a more fitting focal point for community life
than the Sunday celebration of the eucharist.

A reflective and loving participation in the eucharist
remains for most Catholics the single most important way in
which we celebrate and renew and deepen our faith and our
Christian life. The eucharist is a community event. It is an act of
the whole church, of Christ and of his body. It is not something
that we do privately. We leave our individual homes and gather
in a church or some other agreed-upon place. In coming
together out of our relative isolation, we become aware of ourselves as members of a believing community. Everyone else who
has come to this Mass has come for more or less the same reason

we have come. We share the same faith, we experience similar religious and spiritual needs, we are animated by a common hope and longing.

More than anything else the eucharist is a form of prayer. We worship and praise God; we give thanks for the gifts of creation and the gift of Christ; we ask God's forgiveness and help; we pray for others, for our families and friends, for the poor and those who suffer, for political and church leaders. In the eucharist we pray together not just as individuals but as members of God's family.

As much as the whole eucharistic liturgy is permeated by an atmosphere of prayer, it also involves other things. Its first part focuses on scripture. To be a Christian involves a real love and knowledge of the Bible. Vatican II said that it should be at the heart of any serious spiritual life. In the eucharist it is proclaimed within the community of faith and within its liturgy. We are invited to listen to it as if God and Christ were speaking to us through the human authors and through the voice of the reader. The language of the scriptures may on occasion seem archaic and difficult to understand, but God's voice echoes through them nonetheless. It calls us to conversion, it promises forgiveness, it proclaims the saving reality of Christ. In the gospels we hear Jesus himself inviting us to follow him, to renew our commitment to a life of discipleship. The homily is meant to serve the biblical readings and to help us bring them alive in terms of our own situation, our own experiences.

At the heart of the Mass is the great eucharistic prayer. The priest invites us to join with him in lifting up our hearts and giving praise and thanks to God. The singing of the Sanctus reminds us that our prayer is somehow caught up in and accompanied by the prayer of the angels and saints in heaven. No matter how modest our gathering or simple our surroundings, in the eucharist we participate in the prayer and praise of all of creation.

As the eucharistic prayer continues the priest begs God to send the gift of the Spirit upon the bread and wine and upon the assembled community so that they and we might be transformed into the body of Christ. The recitation of the words of Jesus at the last supper reminds us of the most central truth and reality of our faith: This is my body, my person, given for you; this is my blood poured out for your salvation. The life and mission of Jesus can be summed up in terms of self-giving love. His love reveals the mystery of divine love. In the eucharist we make memory of, we render present among us, the power for forgiveness and life of the sacrificial love of Jesus. Here is our ultimate motive for giving thanks. Here is the meaning of our lives and the ground of our hope.

The eucharistic prayer ends with a great doxology. We offer glory and honor and praise to the Father with, through, and in Christ and in the power of the Spirit. Through the Spirit we are united to Christ and to his sacrifice and prayer; with and through him we offer them to God. It is not by chance that it is in this context we recite together the Our Father. God is not my father and your father and the father of this-or-that person but truly *our* Father. The plural underlines once again the corporate nature of our faith.

Catholics have always insisted on the *real presence.* Christ truly comes to us in the consecrated bread and wine. He comes to us precisely in the act of his self-giving love. To come forward and to receive the eucharist is to proclaim publicly that we want to be caught up into the life and the love of Jesus. We come to be healed and forgiven but we come also for the food and strength we need in order to lead a life of genuine discipleship.

If the moment of our gathering as a community of faith on Sunday morning is an important one in reaffirming our Catholic identity, so also is the moment of our dispersal. The eucharist is something out of the ordinary, something special, a taste of heaven, but it is also meant to have an impact on the way we live here and now. When we come to the eucharist we bring our lives—our sorrows and hopes, our joys and fears. We bring all that we are and unite ourselves with the life and self-offering of Jesus. Through communion we hope that we in some way will be transformed. We hope that we will return to everyday life with our faith deepened and our commitment renewed and our desire to serve others strengthened. Ideally, the eucharist and the yearly cycle of its celebration should lead us to an ever-deepening experience of God and of Christ and to an ever more authentically Christian way of life.

THE PRIORITY OF GRACE

To many outsiders the Catholic Church seems to be marked by a great deal of ritual and doctrine, a very developed and detailed moral code, and an extensive pattern of church law. The emphasis in all this on rules and regulations is seen as a key factor in what is widely perceived as a distinctively Catholic preoccupation with guilt. As understandable to some degree as such perceptions are, they miss what is far more important, what is in fact at the heart of Catholic life. They miss the absolute priority that Catholicism gives to the reality of grace.

The word *grace* suggests a gift. It points to the graciousness of all God's activities in our regard. Creation itself is a gift. Freely and out of love God calls into being what is not God in order finally to share the divine life with spiritual creatures. It is this invitation to share the life of God that Catholicism has always understood as the highest form of grace. The invitation is not something static, nor is it given once and for all. It is woven into the very texture of our lives. It has a history, a history that corresponds both to the unfolding of our individual lives and to the overall sweep of human history.

Some years ago my mother had a debilitating stroke; it condemned her to a dramatically reduced existence in a chronic-care hospital. I became deeply involved with her and tried to the extent that I could to make the final year of her life less destructive of her dignity and identity than it otherwise might have been. It was a difficult year for her and for me, and yet when it was over and I reflected on what it had meant for both of us the phrase "a time of grace" spontaneously came to mind. What I meant by that was that in and through the suffering and the struggle and the pain, good things happened, good for her, good for me, and good for others as well. As a person of faith I saw these good things as a manifestation of God's gracious and healing presence in the midst of what in so many ways was a profoundly negative experience. As so often in Christian life, the paradox of death and resurrection, of sorrow and joy, of failure and success was at work. If Christ proclaims the reality of God's love and the final triumph of goodness and life, he himself encountered rejection and death. The cross is a part of life. We experience failure and limits, we suffer and die, and yet even as we do we know in faith and by meditation on the destiny of Jesus that these things are not the final word. Good Friday gives way to Easter Sunday. God's graciousness in our regard is present in a particularly intense way in the midst of what otherwise seems darkness and defeat.

Catholics tend to have a special devotion to Mary, the mother of Jesus, a devotion that has taken a variety of forms at different times and in different cultures. More than anything else Mary gives concrete and human expression to the Catholic understanding of grace. This has been brought out in particular by the two doctrines about Mary that have been adopted as official church teaching in the modern period, the immaculate conception and the assumption, defined respectively in 1854 and 1950. Both proclaim the graciousness of God to Mary and indirectly to all of humanity. The salvation brought through Christ is meant to overcome the destructive power of sin, our individual sins as well as of that situation of sin that has been the human lot since the sin of our first parents. It is God's way of healing us from within and setting us once again on the road to becoming the kind of creatures that God intended us to be from the beginning. The dogma of the immaculate conception affirms that in Mary's case God's graciousness enveloped her from the first instance of her existence, making her then and throughout her life a privileged temple of the Holy Spirit and a special friend in whom divine wisdom dwelt.

The teaching about the assumption proclaims that Mary was caught up body and soul into the triumph of the resurrection of Jesus. God's graciousness extends to our bodies and with them to the whole of created reality. In a way that we cannot imagine, we are invited to hope that our life and the life of humanity will be brought to fulfillment in and through the paschal mystery of Christ. In Mary that fulfillment has already begun. Her destiny is for us a sign of hope.

When Catholics pray the Hail Mary or contemplate a statue or painting of, for example, Mary and the Child, they cannot but be struck by the goodness and graciousness, the gentleness and kindness of God. The liturgy has traditionally applied to Mary texts from the Bible referring to divine wisdom. It is almost as if in practice Mary has been experienced as a manifestation, an embodiment of the feminine side of God.

At the same time Mary is a human being like us. She was invited by God to play an active role in the story of salvation. In her faith and commitment we see a model and pattern for our own lives. The triumph of God's grace in her offers a suggestion, a paradigm, of how that same grace might be operative in us. God respects our freedom and invites our cooperation.

What is embodied in devotion to Mary is brought out in a different way in the traditional Catholic emphasis on the sacraments. We have already mentioned baptism and confirmation and above all the eucharist. To them can be added reconciliation and the sacrament of the anointing of the sick as well as marriage and ordination. Although all of them require a human response, the Catholic tradition has always seen in them very special channels of God's grace. It is one thing to pray for God's help and blessing as two people commit themselves to one another in marriage. It is another thing for them to believe that their mutual commitment and the life that flows from it is itself a sacrament, a sign and symbol of God's healing and loving presence in the midst of their life. In marriage as in everything else the priority rests with God, with God's love, with God's gift and grace.

A few years ago a former classmate of mine was dying of cancer. As the seriousness of her condition became evident, I suggested that we celebrate with her family and friends the sacrament of the anointing of the sick. It took place in her home within the context of the eucharist. The occasion turned out to be deeply moving; it brought out much that is best in the Catholic sacramental tradition. We were conscious of ourselves as a "domestic church." There was a sense of the presence of Christ in the word, in the anointing, in the eucharist, and in our small but loving and supportive community. It was a healing and peace-giving presence. My friend's faith seemed strengthened and her courage renewed. Something of the same nature happened for the rest of us. For everyone who took part it was a moment of grace.

A living faith in the priority of God's grace does not excuse us from struggle and effort. Quite the contrary. What it does do, however, is help us to understand that what we do is secondary; it is a response to a prior gift, it is not the be-all and the end-all that in and of itself has to create meaning and make our lives worthwhile. To have a sense of grace is to have a sense that we have been loved into existence, that we have a dignity and a destiny that we could never give ourselves, and that no one can ever take from us. No matter what our gifts, no matter what we achieve in life, we are graced by God in Christ and through the Spirit. We are called to live in God's presence and to experience God's healing and renewing Spirit within us.

THE MEANING OF DISCIPLESHIP

If Catholicism recognizes the priority in Christian life of grace, it also understands and emphasizes the necessity of our response to God's gift. When Jesus proclaimed the good news of the in-breaking of God's reign, he invited his hearers to faith and conversion. Faith here implies an openness to God, a recognition that God exists, and that in and through the life, message, and destiny of Jesus God has drawn close to us offering forgiveness and reconciliation and the possibility of a new and renewed life. Conversion suggests a change of mind and heart, a turning toward God and a willingness to walk in God's ways.

The development of the RCIA and in particular the emphasis that it puts on a period of serious preparation for baptism underlines the importance of our response to God's offer. The catechumenate is meant to provide those wishing to be baptized with an opportunity to test and deepen their faith and to begin to live a genuinely Christian life. Adult baptism requires a profession of faith and a sincere desire to reject evil and sin and to embrace the values and the vision of the gospel.

One of the most traditional terms for describing the way of life that believers are invited to embrace is *discipleship*. In the New Testament the word refers initially to those who responded to the call of Jesus and literally followed after him, as students at that time might have followed a teacher. By extension the term came to be applied to those who after the resurrection accepted in faith the preaching of the apostles and joined the community of believers. Serious Christians desire to follow Jesus in their own concrete situation, to lead a life inspired by his example and his teaching. It is for this reason that the gospels—with their accounts of the life as well as of the teaching of Jesus—remain the single most important source of inspiration for committed Christians.

Jesus offers a remarkable example of faith and fidelity. The God whom he addressed as Father was at the center of his life. Jesus received a mission from God, and everything he did served it. In spite of rejection, misunderstanding, abandonment, and suffering, he remained faithful unto the end. In doing so he showed his extraordinary love for us. "Christ loved us and gave himself for us, a fragrant offering and sacrifice to God" (Eph 5:3). Jesus seems to have had a special love for the poor and the marginalized. He ate with outcasts and sinners and challenged the wealthy to be sensitive to those in need. He has been described as "a man for others."

The Sermon on the Mount (Mt 5–7) has often been seen as offering a summary of the ethical teaching of Jesus. The emphasis in it is on love of neighbor, love even of those who hate and perse-cute us. The beatitudes with which the sermon begins suggest the attitudes and values that Jesus most wanted to see reflected in his followers. He declares blessed are the meek and the merciful, those who hunger for justice, and those who work for peace.

Over the centuries Christian preachers and thinkers have tried to synthesize in various ways all that is involved in Christian discipleship. In addition to the beatitudes they have pointed to a famous incident in the gospels where Jesus sums up the Mosaic and indeed all moral law in terms of the twofold commandment of love of God and of neighbor. In these two commandments, Jesus says, one can find a summary of teaching of both the law and the prophets. The commandment of love remains today *the* fundamental law of Christian and Catholic life. What it implies in the concrete in any given situation is not always easy to dis-cern. And yet it remains the deepest truth about the life to which in Christ we are called. God is love and wants to share that love with us. God has loved us into existence and in an even more remarkable manifestation of love has sent the eternal Son to rec-oncile and heal us and to bring us back into friendship with God.

Because God is love, what God wants from us more than anything else is love in return. What is entailed in loving God, however, is not always clear; we rarely deal directly with God. One way of loving God is by loving God's creation, by loving in a special way those creatures who are made in God's image and likeness and with whom we share a common life and a common destiny. To love God means to want to fulfill God's plan, God's hope for us and the world. To love God is also to praise and worship God and to give thanks for all God's gifts.

The parable of the Good Samaritan reminds us that the neighbor of whom Jesus speaks is not to be understood narrowly. The outsider, the one who at first glance has little to do with us, has to be included in our love. What perhaps defines those whom from Jesus' point of view we are to love in a special way is their need. At the end, he makes clear, we will be judged on whether or not we have reached out to the hungry and the naked, to the sick and the imprisoned, and more generally, to those who are weak and vulnerable. The first letter of John, a document that both emphasizes the importance of love and affirms that God is love, is realistic about our love of God. "Those who say, 'I love God,' and hate their brothers or sisters, are liars; for those who do not love a brother or sister whom they have seen, cannot love God whom they have not seen" (1 Jn 4:20). Jesus says that what we do or fail to do for those in need, we do or fail to do for him (Mt 25:31–46).

CHRISTIAN ETHICS

The Catholic tradition has always put great emphasis on clarifying issues of ethics or morality. If it has found its deepest inspiration and insight in the scriptures, it has not hesitated to learn from other sources as well. It has tried to integrate the best in the ethical understanding and practice of humanity with the teaching of Jesus. In the ancient church this meant taking over a good deal of the teaching about virtues that had been developed in Greek and Roman culture. Thomas Aquinas structured his vision of the Christian moral life in terms of certain fundamental attitudes and dispositions known as the *cardinal virtues:* prudence, justice, fortitude, and temperance. The more God-related aspects of Christian life Aquinas brought together under the general headings of faith, hope, and love. In every area he saw a coming together of God's gift and of our response. God grants grace but we are called to cooperate with it, to respond to it, to commit ourselves actively to a way of life inspired by it. The language of virtue suggests that the Christian life involves a process. We gradually become just and courageous by performing acts of justice and courage. The repetition of good acts disposes us in such a way that over time such actions become all but second nature to us. Someone encouraged in childhood to be responsible, for example, and who subsequently tries to make such an attitude his or her own will in all likelihood be a responsible adult.

If the virtues already suggest some of the concrete areas in which ethical or moral decisions have to be made and actions undertaken, a further traditional way in which the specifics of Christian morality have been developed is by an appeal to the Ten Commandments. In the Bible the commandments are presented as in some way a condition imposed on the Israelites by the covenant that God has sealed with them. Through Moses the God of exodus and salvation invites the people into a special relationship: "I will take you as my people, and I will be your God" (Ex 6:7). As such they must obey God's commandments. In the Sermon on the Mount Jesus makes it clear that he has not come to abolish the commandments but rather to bring them to a kind of fulfillment. In comparison with the commandment which forbad murder, Jesus says: "But I say to you that if you are angry with a brother or sister, you will be liable to judgment; and if you insult a brother or sister, you will be liable to the council; and if you say 'You fool,'" you will be liable to the hell of fire" (Mt 5:22).

There is no room in the present context to go into any detail in regard to a Catholic understanding of morality. The recently published *Catechism of the Catholic Church* outlines much that is involved here under the individual commandments. Although some of the latter are formulated negatively, the emphasis in the catechism is clearly positive; it tries to spell out the major areas of our moral responsibility. In doing so it offers us enormous help in fulfilling one of the major requirements for growth in the

Christian life—the formation of conscience. If our conscience is the final judge of whether or not we should or should not do this or that action, we have a responsibility to continue throughout life to grow in our understanding and appreciation of ethical issues and of the concrete implications of discipleship. Because Catholicism stresses the community dimension of Christianity and because it understands the church to be graced with a teaching authority, it emphasizes the role that the pope and the bishops and the traditional teaching of the church have in helping us in this regard. With scientific and technological developments in the area of medicine, to take but one example, new ethical issues have arisen that challenge the most intelligent and best willed among us. Here the role of the magisterium is to help Catholics to recognize the implications of traditional principles in radically changed circumstances. It also alerts us to issues and values to which we might be insensitive or that in our culture might be particularly vulnerable to being undermined. In this regard the pope in recent years has stressed the importance of integrating sexuality into our ethical and spiritual lives. It is a precious gift of God that within marriage can be a means to and an expression of the most profound love.

Catholic leaders at every level stress the dignity and value of human life. This extends from the unborn child to elderly and seriously ill persons. Catholicism, however, is not only against abortion and euthanasia, but it is strongly committed to fostering life at every stage of its existence. This attitude comes out in a special way in the development in our century of Catholic social teaching.

To be a Catholic is to belong to a community of faith. The RCIA, as we saw, underlines the community dimension of Christian initiation and challenges all Catholics to deepen the communal sense of their faith. To the degree that we do so we cannot help but become more sensitive to the social dimension of all life. We are not isolated individuals. We belong to a family, a church, a nation, to the whole of humanity. Almost everything about Catholicism is meant to deepen our social sensitivity. Both creation and redemption proclaim the solidarity that is meant to exist among people. Christian discipleship today cannot stop at the personal level. If we are to love our neighbor in a world as complex as ours, then we must be concerned about social issues, structures, and institutions, and about whether or not or to what degree they foster life at all its levels or threaten or even destroy it. The issues are difficult and demanding; here again Catholics have help in trying to address them in the social teaching of the church.

CELEBRATING FORGIVENESS AND RECONCILIATION

The more seriously we take the gift of grace and the challenge of discipleship the more acutely aware we become of how little we appreciate and foster the one and live up to the other. Imperfection, failure, and sin are part of our life. This is the reason that at the beginning of each eucharist we recall our need for God's mercy. Sometimes, however, we recognize that more is required. We need to admit our guilt to an ordained representative of the church and to hear in his words the assurance of God's forgiveness. The sacrament of reconciliation is an important part of Catholic life. It brings the sacramental nature of the church to bear on our individual and collective sinfulness. The power for reconciliation and healing let loose in the world through the death and resurrection of Jesus continues to meet us on our journey, not only in the eucharist but also in the sacrament of forgiveness. It too is grace; it too challenges us to newness of life.

The new rites for reconciliation include two communal forms: one involves general absolution, and the other does not. In both cases a community of believers gathers for the celebration of the sacrament. There are appropriate readings and a homily and a common expression of contrition and penance. Such rituals add to the private form of confession an awareness of the social dimension of both sin and forgiveness. A sense of solidarity is central to Catholic life. What we are and what we do have implications for others. Positive activity and personal growth in holiness cannot but have a positive effect on the whole church. Failure and sin, on the other hand, always in one form or another undermine the efforts of others. In the communal ritual we become aware of this fact and seek forgiveness not only from God but from one another. In the early church reconciliation was widely known as the *peace of the church.* It involved renewing and deepening membership in the community of faith.

In reconciliation, as in all the sacraments, the church expresses itself and brings to bear on individual members and specific communities the resources that are within it. In this sacrament we experience the church itself as a reconciled and a reconciling community. The Spirit that is the source of its life and energy is a Spirit of forgiveness and of healing.

LIVING IN HOPE

The liturgical renewal coming out of Vatican II has brought an important shift in our understanding of the eucharist. Prior to the council the most common way for Catholics to speak of the eucharist was to refer to it as the sacrifice of the Mass. That term evoked more than anything else the suffering and death of Jesus on the cross. That once-and-for-all sacrifice by which he had won salvation was in some way rendered present on the altar under the appearances of bread and wine. This emphasis tended to be reinforced by the dominant place given to the crucifix in most churches. It underlined in a powerful, visual way the teaching of the catechism about the sacrificial nature of the Mass.

The new liturgy in no sense denies the traditional teaching, but it does remind us that the cross of Jesus is inseparable from the resurrection. The death and resurrection *together* constitute the paschal mystery, the saving event by which God through Christ has brought about forgiveness and reconciliation and offered us the possibility of a new life. In the eucharist we make memory of the whole of that saving event. In the eucharistic prayer, after the words of Jesus over the bread and wine are recited, we are invited to proclaim the mystery of our faith. Although different formulations are possible, mention is ordinarily made of the death, resurrection, and future coming of Christ at the end of time. The Christ who is present in the eucharist and who invites us to join with him in his praise and worship of God is not the dead but the living Christ. Faith in the resurrection brings to the eucharist and to the whole of Christian life a profound sense of hope. God raised Jesus from the dead and in doing so both gave eternal validity to his life and death and revealed the ultimate basis for our hope. Analogous to the rainbow in the story of Noah, the resurrection remains for Christians a sign of God's final intention in regard to the whole of human life. It proclaims the definitive triumph of life over death and of goodness over evil.

Every eucharist renews and deepens our hope, but this is particularly true in the case of the new liturgy for Christian burial. Until the recent changes the emphasis in funerals was on death and judgment. The use of black vestments and ornaments gave symbolic expression to the sense of loss and mourning. The prayers stressed the fearful seriousness of death and of the soul's encounter in and through it with God. The *Dies irae* ("day of wrath") evoked the final judgment and the fires of hell.

Although the new liturgy in no sense makes light of death or of the need the dead have of our prayers as they pass from this life into God, it does bring out that death represents for the person of faith the final stage of a journey begun in baptism. At the very outset of our Christian lives we were brought for the first time into contact with the saving and healing power of Christ's death and resurrection. The whole of a person's spiritual life involves a continuing and deepening passage from self-centeredness and sin to an attitude of faith and love. The paschal mystery for each one of us is brought to its fulfillment in our final passage through death into the life of God. Because we make this passage with and in Christ and animated by his Spirit, we make it in hope.

Hope should be a distinguishing feature of the life of a Catholic. Almost everything in the church and especially in its liturgy is there to remind us of the reasons for our hope. The key here, as elsewhere, is our sense of God. Creation itself gives us a basis for hope. If God freely and lovingly has called us into being, then surely it is not to abandon us to chance or self-destructiveness. The God who made us has a plan for us and will give us what we need to play our part in it. This does not mean that we will not suffer or fail or repeatedly encounter our limits; it means rather that God will be with us in the midst of such experiences and will give us the faith and courage to discern the presence of grace even there.

The conviction that God is with us is central to biblical faith. God is both the creator and the Lord of human history. God responds to the prayer of the oppressed and intervenes in order to liberate them from slavery. The presence of God in the midst of humanity reaches a new level of intensity, a new visibility in the person and life of Jesus. He is in a unique way Emmanuel, God with us. In Jesus, God embraces a human life and in doing so comes close to and renews the dignity of each and every human being. Here is a second and all but unimaginable basis for hope. God not only created us, but the Word and Wisdom of God became human to reinforce our dignity and to enable us to share in God's own life.

The time of Jesus was a privileged moment in human history. Although in one sense it ended with his death and resurrection, in another sense it continues today. At the end of Matthew's gospel the risen Christ promises to be with his disciples until the end of time (Mt 28:20). In the other gospels and in Paul the presence of Jesus is related to the gift of the Spirit. Through the Spirit the risen Christ continues to be active in the community of faith and in the world. The time of the church is in a special way the time of the Spirit. The Spirit of Christ is a Spirit of truth and love, of fidelity and service, of faith and hope. It is ultimately the Spirit, the Spirit of God and of Christ, alive and active in our hearts, in the church, and in the world who is the immediate source of our hope.

Christian hope is above all hope in God, in God precisely as revealed and active among us in Christ and through the Spirit. Persons of hope have a deep conviction that their life is worthwhile, that it is meaningful, that it is going somewhere and that its goal is not negation but fulfillment. In its broadest form, hope has to do with the definitive transformation and salvation of our lives in God. Death is not simply an end but rather a threshold into a new and higher life. If that is our ultimate hope, it does not exhaust all the things for which we hope. We have hopes in regard to this life as well. We hope for an experience of meaning and of joy, for a certain amount of happiness and love, for a sense of achievement. Similarly, we hope not only for ourselves but for others—for our family and friends, for our country, for the world, for all of God's creation. Christian hope is as all-encompassing as Christian faith and Christian love.

The opposite of hope is despair. It breeds passivity and indifference and cynicism. The more despair invades our heart the more difficult action becomes. Despair undermines the will to act. If there is no hope of achieving something, why should we bother to try to do so? Christian hope does not allow itself to be undermined by difficulty or even failure. The cross teaches us to hope against hope. Through failure and suffering and death God redeemed the world and in doing so revealed the paradoxical ways that lead to life and fulfillment.

We live in an increasingly secular world, a world where along with much that is good there is obviously a great deal that is enormously destructive. Violence and greed and the most crass kind of self-seeking are all around us. The church itself at times seems on the verge of losing its identity and integrity. Hope is not blind to such things. And yet it continues to trust and to work. It trusts in the presence of God among us and in doing so it overcomes defeatism and bitterness. It renews our energy and enables us to begin again.

Catholics share with everyone else a common humanity with all that that entails. Beyond that we are religious persons with a sense of the mystery of life and of God. With other Christians we profess a common faith in Christ and in the reconciling and healing presence of his Spirit in the midst of the world. What is perhaps most distinctive of us as Catholics is our membership in the church with everything that it involves in terms of liturgy and sacraments, of mutual help and support. The faith of Catholics embraces God and the world and the meaning of human life. The love to which we are called reaches out to both God and neighbor. It has social as well as personal dimensions. Hope colors everything that we do. It defines our attitude in the face of suffering and death. It motivates us to work for our families and for the betterment of the world. It encourages us to become actively involved in the life and mission of the church. In spite of current difficulties, tensions, and challenges, the church remains central to our faith and is a special object of our love and of our hope.